Queer

Susan Stryker

Perverted Passions from the Golden Age of the Paperback

Pulp

CHRONICLE BOOKS
SAN FRANCISCO

Acknowledgments

This book grew out of an earlier and smaller project, the *Gay Pulp* and *Lesbian Pulp* address books I did for Chronicle Books in 2000. Chronicle liked them; I liked them, and they were well received, so Chronicle asked if I would do a book for them on the history of queer-themed paperbacks. I would like to thank my editor, Alan Rapp, for suggesting that I write *Queer Pulp* and for bearing with me as I scrambled to complete the manuscript not too awfully long after my deadline. Thanks, too, to copy editor Rosana Francescato for her professionalism in cleaning up my prose, and to graphic designer Michael Boland of Watts Design. I extend my gratitude as well to Willie Walker, Terence Kissack, Victor Silverman, Alyson Belcher, Catrina Marchetti, Bob Davis, and Jeanette Minor: you all know what you did. Love as always to Kim, Wilson, and Denali for their wonderful support and welcome distractions from writing. A special tip of the hat to David Modersbach for the use of his family's cabin at Lake Tahoe during the final frantic sprint to the finish.

Permissions

Every effort has been made to trace the ownership of all copyrighted material included in this volume. Any errors that may have occurred are inadvertent and will be corrected in subsequent editions, provided notification is sent to the publisher.

Library of Congress Cataloging-in-Publication Data available.

ISBN 0-8118-3020-9

Printed in Hong Kong.

Distributed in Canada by Raincoast Books
9050 Shaughnessy Street
Vancouver, British Columbia V6P 6E5

10 9 8 7 6 5 4 3 2

Chronicle Books, LLC
85 Second Street
San Francisco, California 94105

www.chroniclebooks.com

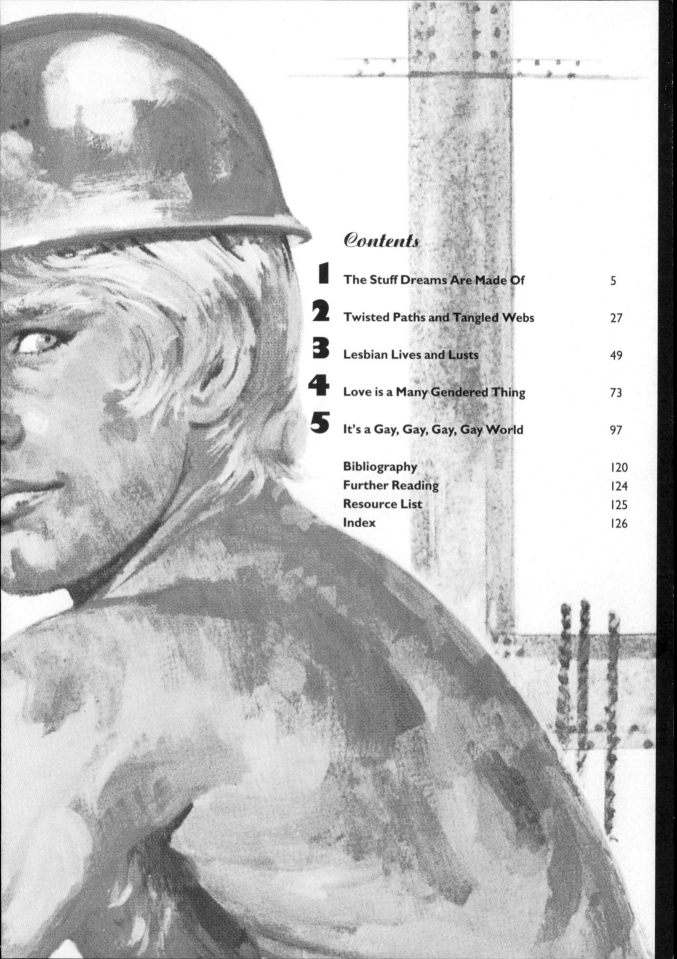

Contents

1 The Stuff Dreams Are Made Of   5

2 Twisted Paths and Tangled Webs   27

3 Lesbian Lives and Lusts   49

4 Love is a Many Gendered Thing   73

5 It's a Gay, Gay, Gay, Gay World   97

Bibliography   120
Further Reading   124
Resource List   125
Index   126

The Stuff Dreams Are Made Of

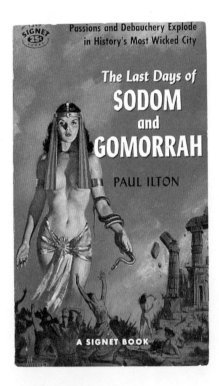

Paul Ilton. *The Last Days of Sodom and Gomorrah*. New York: Signet Books/NAL, 1957.
Sex sells. This nonfiction book by Paul Ilton about a famously wicked city of yore whose name is virtually synonymous with homosexuality received a memorably salacious cover treatment. Ilton's back-cover biography says he led many Near Eastern archeological digs and served as a biblical history consultant for many Hollywood epics. He apparently had an eye for the steamier details of the Holy Writ—a year earlier Signet had published his equally lurid *Secrets of Mary Magdelene*.

Sex sells—and for several decades in the middle of the last century, the immense popularity of paperback books saturated with sexual content proved the truth of that two-bit insight into America's national psyche better than any other mass culture phenomenon.

Offered for sale in bus depots and drugstores rather than book shops catering to a supposedly higher-brow clientele, paperbacks were the transitory and transportable artifacts of an increasingly mobile and uprooted society. Small enough to slip into a purse or jacket pocket, cheap enough to throw away, they were produced for a culture accustomed to ease and hooked on speed—packaged and marketed with the same ad agency acumen that invented streamlined toasters and tail-finned automobiles. Sporting lurid art and breathless blurbs that hawked whatever sensationalistic (or merely sensationalized) story lay between the covers, mid-twentieth-century paperbacks were designed to be seen. They were signs and symptoms of the newfound visibility that sexuality in all its myriad forms achieved in America during the tumultuous years around World War II. Paperbacks were the publishing industry's equivalent of a roadside honky-tonk's neon light, beckoning to lonely travelers on the deserted highways of life.

Mass-market paperback books considerably predated World War II. Book historians point to sixteenth-century Venetian publisher and printer Aldus Manutius as the originator of the form—his Aldine Classics supplied students and scholars with small, inexpensive translations of ancient Greek and Roman authors. Garishly illustrated "penny dreadfuls," "dime novels," and other similar

Truman Capote. *Other Voices, Other Rooms.* **New York: Signet Books/NAL, 1949.**
The "peephole cover" was a popular motif in paperback illustration, by means of which the form of the book itself suggested the voyeuristic function such books often played in shedding light on taboo topics. Capote was one of several young queer Southern authors who achieved mainstream acclaim in the late 1940s. He was only twenty-one when he published *Other Voices, Other Rooms,* written from the viewpoint of a prepubescent adolescent with decidedly gay sensibilities.

diversions catering to the lowest common denominators of literary taste were wildly popular by the middle of the nineteenth century, as were plain but affordable paperback reprints of respected authors' works. The first modern Pocket Books—with their convenient-to-carry trim dimensions, illustrative cover art, paper bindings, and colorfully dyed edges—appeared in 1939, just as the clouds of war were beginning to break in Europe. But it was World War II itself, the largest mobilization of personnel in human history, that transformed the reading habits of the American nation. The military supplied soldiers with slender, lightweight armed services editions of popular literary titles to help relieve the tedium of camp life, thereby fostering the reading habit among millions of young men who otherwise might never have cracked the cover of a more expensive book, and creating as an unintended consequence a vast market for the paperback format.

The war and its aftermath shaped the content of many mid-century paperbacks, just as it had popularized their physical form. Hard-boiled paperback plot lines catered to sentiments haunted by the knowledge of concentration camps and the shadow of the mushroom cloud. They spoke to sensibilities rendered cynical by the hollow and unequally distributed affluence of postwar material culture, and many addressed these concerns in a critical voice or disaffected mood not often witnessed in more polite or officious contexts. Harboring the brooding content that lingered beneath the bright, false, chrome-plated surfaces covering much of postwar American life, paperback books collectively functioned as a vast cultural unconscious. Deposited there were fantasies of fulfillment as well as the desperate yearnings, petty betrayals, unrequited passions, and unreasoning violence that troubled the margins of the longed-for world. Like Dashiell Hammett's Maltese falcon, paperbacks were fashioned from "the stuff dreams are made of."

Hammett's falcon is a jewel-encrusted statuette of a bird that becomes the object of an all-consuming quest undertaken by an assortment of ruthless yet ineffectual criminals. It is pulp literature's most potent symbol of the process through which projected fantasies become concrete and circulate endlessly through the pathways of deferred desire. Like the falcon, too, paperback books coalesced into bona fide fetish items, physical objects invested with the promise of emotional gratification. The popular "peephole" style of cover art, suggesting stolen glimpses into exotic interior territories at once psychological and geographical, literalized the voyeuristic appeal of early postwar paperback art. Through the peephole covers we saw slovenly white trash swamp-dwellers, libidinous inner-city Blacks, suburban

Harboring the brooding content that lingered beneath the bright, false, chrome-plated surfaces covering much of postwar American life, paperback books collectively functioned as a vast cultural unconscious.

Deposited there were fantasies of fulfillment as well as the desperate yearnings, petty betrayals, unrequited passions, and unreasoning violence that troubled the margins of the longed-for world.

wife-swappers, lesbian girl-gangs, and other such denizens of the dominant culture's overheated imagination. Featuring eye-grabbing illustrations of primal scenes blatantly displayed in the public sphere, the covers seduced readers with the imagined pleasures and forbidden knowledge within. They supplied a porous, emotionally charged, two-way boundary between the hidden and the seen. Born from a seamless fusion of form and function, paperbacks became near-perfect commodities—little machines built to incite desire at the point of purchase, capture it, and drive it repeatedly into the cash nexus at 25 cents a pop.

Sexuality, of course, is the privileged content of the unconscious domain, and unconscious sexuality is by definition polymorphously perverse: it goes where it wants and not where you will it, flowing like water into available forms. Sometimes it courses through channels worn smooth by tradition; sometimes it wells up and overflows its accustomed boundaries to cut new pathways toward pleasure. Wayward sexuality is what mid-century paperbacks peddled par excellence. Not every paperback, of course—the format lent itself promiscuously to all sorts of content right from the start, from Shakespeare and Pearl Buck to Dale Carnegie's *How to Win Friends and Influence People* to the latest Agatha Christie mystery. But paperbacks in the 1940s and '50s were undoubtedly the venue of choice for exploring and exploiting certain taboo topics

disallowed in movies and radio and the pages of reputable hardcover books. Before the sexual revolution of the 1960s and the explosion of soft- and hard-core pornographic magazines that came in its wake, paperback books were pretty much the only game in town when it came to explicit portrayals of sexuality in the mass media.

Not every paperback that delved into eyebrow-raising material contained individual characters or acts labeled perverse in the sanctimonious terms of the day—though enough did to fill the pages of *Queer Pulp*. Rather, the paperback field as a whole was perverse in a more general and diffuse way, somewhat in the manner of dreams that refuse to censor desire when it strays toward socially unsanctioned ends. Mid-twentieth-century paperbacks mapped a world of loose women and lost men who wandered in a moral twilight, a world of sin and sex and drugs and booze and every ugly thing human beings could conspire to do to one another. It was a world in which bisexual experimentation, like a single puff from a marijuana cigarette, often served as a first step on a long and sordid journey that tended toward heroin addiction, murder, homosexuality, the breakdown of gender distinctions, and the certain madness that lay beyond. In the dark night of cities both real and imagined, straight-laced America held a paperback mirror up to its face and found a queer reflection peering back. Queer folk hungry for recognition

Maureen McKernan. *The Amazing Crime and Trial of Leopold and Loeb.* **New York: Signet Books/ NAL, 1957.**
Public anxiety about the "social problem" of homosexuality in the years after World War II persuaded publishers to dredge up decades-old stories with queer content—like this rehash of the notorious Leopold and Loeb gay murder trial of the 1920s. The story was filmed at least twice—once as *Compulsion* (based on a novelization of the same name by Meyer Levin), and more famously by Alfred Hitchcock as *Rope.* Note the cover's Rorschach test inkblot on a purple background—a subtle visual association of homosexuality with psychopathology.

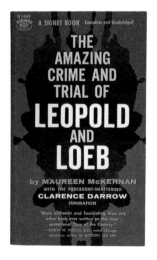

Donald Porter Geddes and Enid Curie. *About the Kinsey Report.* **New York: Signet Books, 1948.** Alfred Kinsey's 1948 stereotype-shattering *Report on Sexuality in the Human Male* (followed a few years later by a companion volume on female sexuality) revealed the wide range of sexual behaviors that American men engaged in—including the startling observation that one man in ten had had repeated homosexual experiences. Robert Jonas—one of the more famous paperback illustrators who was noted for his abstract, nonrealistic cover images—supplied the art for this collection of essays by prominent social scientists discussing the significance of the Kinsey report.

Ray Train. *Miss Kinsey's Report.* **Cleveland, OH: Chevron Publications, 1967.**
In one of the more lurid "sleaze" paperbacks that proliferated in the 1960s, Ray Train offered a porno- graphic account of Alfred Kinsey's fictional sexpot niece, who experi- ences for herself some of the more esoteric practices reported in her famous uncle's books. It was just one indication of the extent to which the Kinsey report shaped popular beliefs about sexuality and contributed to the sexual revolution of the 1960s.

looked in the mirror, too, grimacing or snickering in wry amusement at the distorted images they glimpsed there.

Homosexual feelings are not the only way of differing from the erotic norms of dominant culture, but they certainly occupy a central place in the popular understanding of sexual diversity. Homosexuality attained a new level of visibility in the years following World War II, not just because of the heightened attention to sexuality in general but also because the war itself had helped bring about a new kind of gay and lesbian community. For the first time, the military actively tried to screen out homosexuals during the recruitment and induction process, asking questions about sexual orientation that provided a vocabulary and conceptual framework to many people who might have felt same-sex desires but had never been part of a gay subculture or had the words to express their feelings. The war brought an unprecedented number of people together in sex-segregated settings, which helped foster new gay and lesbian social networks, both in the military itself and in the domestic war industries. When gay people were discovered in the armed services, they were usually discharged in big port cities that served as bases of operation for the military. San Francisco in particular, which served as the principal administrative center for the war in the Pacific, received a disproportionately large share of dishonorably discharged gay service-

men who were in no particular hurry to return to their hometowns. As a result of these wartime developments, homosexual subcultures became much less isolated from one another and much more visible within society at large. This in turn contributed anxious, widespread attention to the "social problem" of homosexuality—a concern frequently reflected in postwar paperback books.

Alfred Kinsey's 1948 *Report on Sexual Behavior in the Human Male* swept aside an older era's conventional assumptions about the heterosexual norm. In the first large statistical survey of modern American sexual practices, Kinsey devised a six-point scale for sexual behavior that ranged from strictly homosexual to strictly heterosexual, and he found that most people fell somewhere between the two. About a third of American men had had at least one homosexual experience, and about one in ten had had multiple encounters. At a moment in American history when homosexuality was already a front-burner issue, Kinsey's report added fuel to the fire. It helped establish the sheer fact of sexual diversity in the public's consciousness and laid an important foundation for the sexual revolution of the 1960s. A few years later, his report on female sexuality had a similar effect on popular knowledge of American women's erotic lives.

Even at the height of antihomosexual hysteria during the most overwrought days of the Cold War, a

W. Somerset Maugham. *Stranger in Paris.* **New York: Bantam Books, 1949.**
This story by celebrated British writer, spy, world traveler, and bon vivant was originally published in 1939 under the title *Christmas Holiday.* A severe stutterer as well as a gay man, Maugham drew on his personal experiences of difference from the mainstream to hone his uniquely urbane and satirical commentary on modern Western society.

Robert McAlmon. *There Was a Rustle of Black Silk Stockings.* **New York: Belmont Books, 1963.**
Considered by some critics to be one of the great "undiscovered" writers of modernist literature, McAlmon ran in the same American expatriate circles in Paris as Ernest Hemingway and Gertrude Stein—both of whom he published early in their careers. *Rustle of Black Silk Stockings,* a collection of four short stories revolving around gay and lesbian characters, had originally been published in France in 1925 under the title *Distinguished Air (Grim Fairy Tales).*

number of paperbacks appeared that dealt with male homosexuality. Most were tarted-up reprints of hardcover novels that earned their authors serious literary reputations. W. Somerset Maugham was perhaps the classiest writer of the lot. Born in Paris to well-heeled British parents but orphaned at an early age, Maugham's severe stutter and homosexual inclinations ruled out for him the career in law that had made his father's fortune. But he turned his sense of difference from the dominant culture in a literary direction, winning widespread fame for his pioneering treatment of physical disability in *Of Human Bondage*. The witty and sophisticated author of dozens of novels, plays, essay collections, travel stories, and memoirs, Maugham also served as a British spy in World War I, inspiring the creation of his friend Ian Fleming's most famous fictional character, James Bond.

Robert McAlmon, a brilliant but lesser-known member of the "lost generation" set that included modernist luminaries like Fitzgerald, Hemingway, and Stein, was another serious author who wrote on homosexual themes and whose work received the pulp treatment at the hands of paperback publishers. Other hardcover authors of paperback reprints ran the gamut from James Cain—one of the original tough-guy writers of hard-boiled crime fiction, whose novel *Serenade* was set in Tijuana's "pansy" scene—to Clarkson Crane, a bohemian littérateur on the English Department faculty at the University of California at Berkeley, whose books cast a knowing eye on the San Francisco Bay Area's sexual underground.

Because of the publishing industry's inherent sexism, lesbians had a more difficult time breaking into the ranks of the established authors than did gay men, but surprisingly, lesbian books played an even larger role in the paperback reprint trade than did books with gay male themes. Lesbian-themed works were also among the most commercially successful titles commissioned specifically for first-time publication in mass-market paperback form. Many of these supposedly low-quality lesbian paperback originals—"PBOs," in the jargon of contemporary paperback collectors—were actually quite successful as literature and represent a significant contribution to mid-twentieth-century American culture. They provided an important outlet for a handful of lesbian writers whose work otherwise might never have seen print. Their unprecedented and unexpected success led later paperback fans to label the period between the mid-1940s and the mid-1960s, when these lesbian PBOs flourished, as a "golden age" for the representation of sexual diversity in mass-market paperbacks.

A few mainstream novels of the immediate postwar period included overtly gay minor characters, offering them to readers as a commentary on the newly perceived prevalence of homosexuality in society. Charles Gorham's 1948 *The Gilded Hearse* chronicles a day in the life of an up-and-coming young editor at an aggressive commercial publisher in Manhattan. The story, billed as a tale of "Love and Ambition—from Dawn to Dawn" was set during one

At a moment in American history when homosexuality was already a front-burner issue, Kinsey's report added fuel to the fire. It helped establish the sheer fact of sexual diversity in the public's consciousness and laid an important foundation for the sexual revolution of the 1960s.

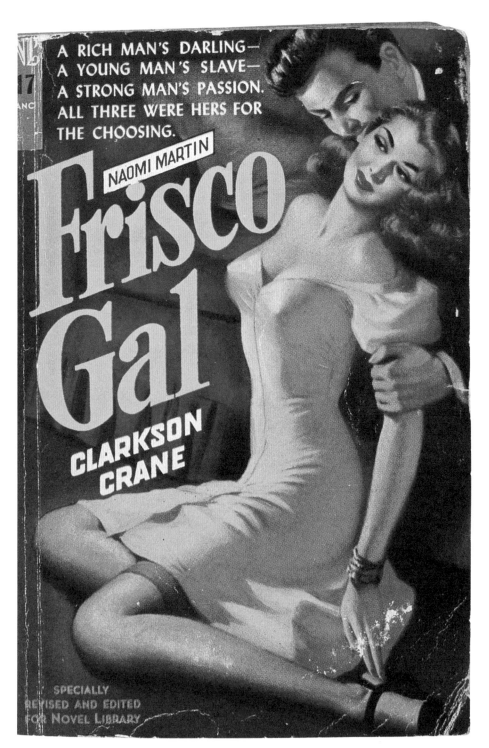

Clarkson Crane. *Frisco Gal.* **New York: Diversey Publishing, 1949.**
Crane was an English professor at the University of California at Berkeley who specialized in California's literary heritage. His early novel *On Western Shores* dealt with the relationships between a gay Berkeley professor and a group of undergraduates. *Frisco Gal* was just another example of the paperback industry's voracious appetite being fed by a writer whose gay sensibilities informed his more mainstream work.

James M. Cain. *Serenade.* **New York: Signet Books/NAL, 1954 (orig. pub. 1937).**
Cain was one of the original tough-guy writers of hard-boiled crime fiction. In this tale of California musicians enjoying the off-season in Mexico, Cain has his hero admit to a previous homosexual relationship, which eventually motivates a grisly murder.

twenty-four-hour period in late September 1938, the same day as the ill-fated Munich Conference that aimed to appease Hitler's territorial aggressions. Gerald Fatt, a co-worker of the principal character, is obviously homosexual, and his character is intended to show the extent to which homosexuality was simply part of the literary and intellectual milieu of mid-century Manhattan. The book was brought up on obscenity charges, partly as a result of the gay content, but a New York magistrate dismissed the charges.

The Fall of Valor, the second of three mid-1940s novels by Charles Jackson, dealt with male homosexuality in a much more central manner. Jackson won lasting recognition for his first novel, *The Lost Weekend,* which paints a searing portrait of an alcoholic's steady disintegration and suggests that the man's inability to deal with his latent homosexuality lay at the root of his self-destruction. Jackson took the title of his second novel from *Moby Dick,* one of the more blatantly homoerotic works in the American literary canon. In it, he describes the collapsing marriage of a Boston university professor who begins to gradually and reluctantly acknowledge his growing attraction to younger men. A bumbling attempt to court a young marine officer ends disastrously, and the novel closes on a melancholy and unresolved note. Homosexuality also figured briefly in *The Outer Margins,* Jackon's third novel, in which he says of an aspiring writer obsessed with a grisly killing, "It was not for nothing, he thought, that the deepest

secrets at the base of tragic art were homosexuality, incest, and murder."

Novelists like Jackson and Gorham approached homosexuality from the outside, viewing it as an objective phenomenon that had appeared in the American social landscape. But another cohort of writers who found mainstream success in the late '40s and early '50s brought a queer perspective to issues of broad social significance. Probably the most famous of the openly queer mid-century writers was dramatist Tennessee Williams, whose *Glass Menagerie, Streetcar Named Desire, Cat on a Hot Tin Roof, Night of the Iguana, Suddenly Last Summer,* and other works transformed the American stage. Like Williams, most of the others also had Southern roots: prominent examples include Carson McCullers, Truman Capote, and Gore Vidal. McCullers made her mark with her 1940 debut novel, *The Heart Is a Lonely Hunter.* In that work, as well as subsequent efforts like *Reflections in a Golden Eye* and the short story "Ballad of the Sad Café," McCullers dwelt on the inner lives of people who felt estranged from society and unlucky in love—themes for which her queer readership had a special affinity, but that also played to a broader audience.

Homosexuality's tendency to give queer authors an outsider's perspective on mainstream society undoubtedly contributed to the mass-culture success of their work at a time when many people suffered from the alienations and dislocations of modernity—a fact that also helps

---

Charles O. Gorham. *The Gilded Hearse.* **New York: Creative Age Press, 1948.**
One of the minor classics of the hard-boiled genre, Gorham's novel chronicles a day in the life of Richard Stiles Eliot, an up-and-coming editor at a middlebrow Manhattan publishing house, on the eve of World War II. One of Eliot's co-workers is Gerald Fatt, a snobbish, artistic homosexual who represents the niche that people with gay sensibilities had secured for themselves in urban American culture by the 1980s.

Charles Jackson. *The Fall of Valor.* **New York: Lion Books, 1955 (orig. pub. 1946).**
Jackson won lasting fame for his treatment of an alcoholic's painful disintegration in his first novel, *The Lost Weekend,* in which he suggested that the root of his protagonist's bouts with the bottle could be found in his repressed homosexuality. In this, his second novel, Jackson tells the story of an unhappily married college professor who begins to recognize his growing attraction to other men.

Tennessee Williams. *A Streetcar Named Desire.* **New York: Signet/NAL, 1951.**
Tennessee (Thomas Lanier) Williams, born in 1911, was a known homosexual who became one of the most celebrated American playwrights of the twentieth century. New American Library took an atypically high-toned approach to illustrating the Signet edition of William's *Streetcar Named Desire,* using a painting by acclaimed social realist Thomas Hart Benton.

Carson McCullers. *Seven.* **New York: Bantam, 1954.**
One of the most celebrated new authors of mid-twentieth-century America, McCullers wrote her 1940 debut novel, *The Heart Is a Lonely Hunter,* at age twenty-two. Although she herself had a string of women lovers, and although homosexual characters often appeared in her work, McCullers's stories were not primarily about gay life. Rather, she wrote about the irrationality of love and the ways that the loneliness of unrequited love can generate strange and intense inner worlds.

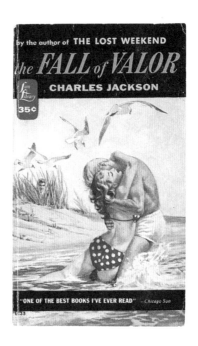

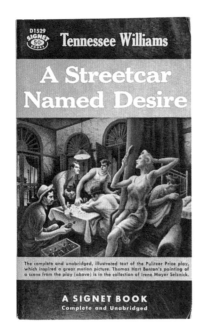

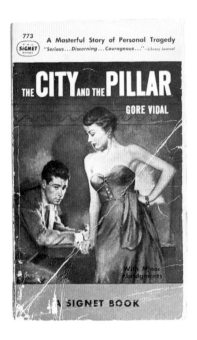

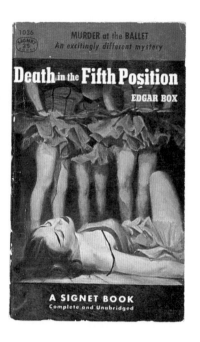

explain the popularity of Southern writers, because the South had a long intellectual tradition of critiquing modern industrial Yankee culture. This was certainly the case with the precocious Truman Capote, whose *Other Voices, Other Rooms* expressed the surreal absurdity of life from the perspective of a thirteen-year-old Mississippian modeled on the adolescent Capote himself. A Southern heritage also informed the sensibilities of Gore Vidal, whose maternal relatives are the politically powerful Gore family of Tennessee. Vidal's *The City and the Pillar* created a scandal as the first postwar novel to focus on a well-adjusted, unapologetic, openly gay adult man who was not killed off at the end of the story for crimes against nature and the social order. Vidal was subsequently blacklisted, and he wrote his next several books under pseudonyms before reestablishing his reputation and emerging as one of the most successful literary figures of the twentieth century.

The same ability to address the malaise of mid-century life that boosted the careers of Vidal, Capote, McCullers, and Williams also contributed to the success of Paul Bowles, a gay New York native and longtime resident of Morocco. His existentialist masterpiece *The Sheltering Sky* made Modern Library's "Top 100 Novels of the 20th Century" list. The story is set in the Sahara Desert and deals with three Americans searching for the meaning of life in the aftermath of World War II; they die without finding it. Bowles, an accomplished classical composer as well as a writer, became something of a guru for Beat authors in

the 1950s. He hosted the North African sojourns of William Burroughs, Allen Ginsberg, and Jack Kerouac and exerted a formative influence on all of their careers.

The golden era of queer pulps in the mid-twentieth century coincided with the maturation of the science-fiction field, which, like the more established and conventional genres, offered abundant opportunities to express variant attitudes about sexuality and gender and provided work for queer authors. In many respects, the genre was exceptionally well suited to extrapolate from contemporary social concerns and promote visions of alternative societies, new forms of embodiment, and novel pathways for desire and pleasure. Even routine exercises like Frank Long's *Woman From Another Planet* could raise fascinating questions about beings who fell outside the binary gender system that undergirds heterosexuality.

Theodore Sturgeon is widely regarded as the first science-fiction author to regularly and sympathetically explore sexual diversity issues with some degree of insight. His *Venus Plus X* is set in a future utopia that has deliberately eliminated genital difference—much to the consternation of an ordinary human male who is brought into their society. Marion Zimmer Bradley, the science-fiction and fantasy author of such best-sellers as *The Mists of Avalon,* got her start cranking out lesbian potboilers. She introduced queer themes in many books throughout her long career. Samuel Delaney has likewise used science fiction to explore the

---

Gore Vidal. *The City and the Pillar.* **New York: Signet Books/NAL, 1950.**
Vidal broke new literary ground with this unapologetic story of a well-adjusted gay man who doesn't die at the end of the book. It caused quite a scandal in the press and resulted in Vidal being blacklisted by several important reviewers. No matter—he parlayed his bad-boy reputation into a successful career spanning seven decades.

Edgar Box [Gore Vidal]. *Death in the Fifth Position.* **New York: Signet Books, 1953.**
Death in the Fifth Position was one of three routine murder mysteries penned by Gore Vidal in the 1950s under the pseudonym Edgar Box, after he had been blacklisted for his frank and positive representation of homosexual themes in *The City and the Pillar.*

Paul Bowles. *The Sheltering Sky.* **New York: Signet Books/NAL, 1951.**
American expatriate Paul Bowles studied music with Aaron Copeland and produced classical compositions of his own before settling in Morocco and winning widespread praise for fiction like *The Sheltering Sky.* This novel about a disintegrating marriage, set against the harsh backdrop of the Sahara Desert, became an existentialist classic in the 1950s and helped shape the sensibilities of Beat writers William Burroughs, Allen Ginsberg, and Jack Kerouac. A filmed version by Bernardo Bertolucci, starring John Malkovitch and Debra Winger, appeared in 1990.

Frank Belknap Long. *Woman from Another Planet.* **N.p.: Chariot Books, 1960.**
Long got his start as a writer in early science-fiction pulp magazines like *Amazing Science* and later wrote a biography of his friend H. P. Lovecraft. *Woman from Another Planet* tells the story of a man who falls in love with a deceptive alien, whose true nature does not fit into the human sexual binary. It offers an excellent example of science fiction's affinity for queer themes, even when not dealing explicitly with homosexual subject matter.

Charles Eric Maine [David McIlwain]. *World Without Men.* **New York: Ace Books, 1958.** In this reactionary account of an all-lesbian society five hundred years in the future, the author vents his spleen about the introduction of birth control pills in mid-twentieth-century America, which he thinks will lead inexorably to a totalitarian government, the demise of the nuclear family, and the extinction of the male sex.

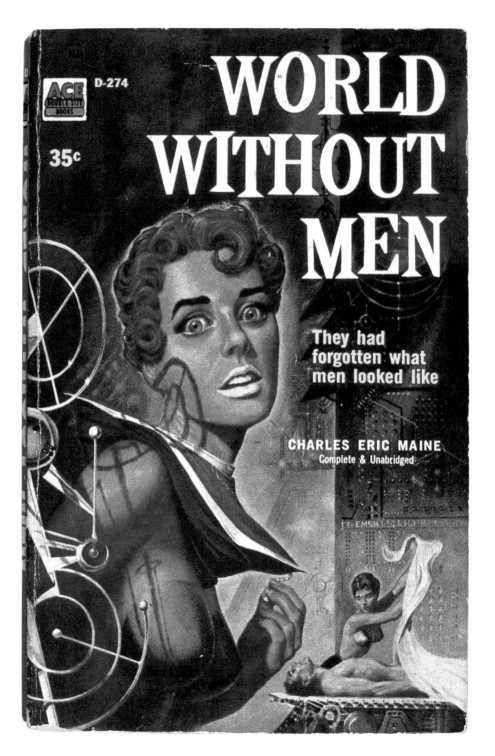

Viewed across the distance of several decades, many mid-twentieth-century paperbacks have lost much of their sexual frisson, and along with it their power to shock or offend.

complex interrelationships between race, gender, and sexuality in a career spanning five decades.

Viewed across the distance of several decades, many mid-twentieth-century paperbacks have lost much of their sexual frisson, and along with it their power to shock or offend. Eric Maine's lesbian-bashing *World Without Men,* a sci-fi cautionary tale about the potentially dire effects of the birth control pill, was probably laughable even when it was published in 1958, but its appeal now is strictly camp. The same is true of Bud Clifton's fictional *Muscle Boy,* a supposed exposé of "Beefcake Kings" who "got their kicks from forbidden feats of strength," including posing nude for naughty pictures intended for a gay male audience. In spite of some tantalizing clues about an actual blackmail ring that existed in San Francisco in the 1950s it commands interest today primarily because of its cover art.

In the 1950s and early 1960s, peddling what were then called "dirty books" could have serious and unfortunate consequences. After the United States Congress turned up the heat with its 1952 hearings into "current pornographic materials," many paperback publishers toned down the most salacious content and cover art. Those who did not—including a growing number of small "sleaze" publishers who deliberately pushed the boundaries of sexually explicit and sexually diverse themes—flirted with disaster. Sanford Aday and his partner Wallace de Ortega Maxey of Fresno, California, were two such publishers who paid heavily for their role in producing racy literature. Aday was a frustrated author who turned

to publishing in 1955, after only two of his ten manuscripts made it into print. He and Maxey—a member of the pioneering gay rights group known as the Mattachine Society—published dozens of books on both gay and straight topics. From their Belmont Avenue address they issued such memorable titles as *I Peddle Jazz, Camera Bait, Our Flesh Was Cheap, Lesbian Twins,* and *His Sex, His Problem* under at least four different imprints—Saber, Fabian, Vega, and National Library Books.

Most of the then-lurid topics exploited by Aday and Maxey would scarcely merit a halfhearted "harrumph" from a church lady nowadays. Although the majority of the books lacked substantial literary merit, they were nevertheless sincere attempts at storytelling. Their characters, plots, and locations were undoubtedly drawn from the obscure, small-town lives of the writers themselves—holy-roller preachers who drank and fornicated and begged forgiveness, aspiring young men who worked their way to college only to be dismissed in a homosexual scandal, smart women with big-city dreams working for small change as taxi dancers in cheap gin joints. A few books were actually diamonds in the rough, like *Sunset* magazine food columnist Lou Hogan's *Gay Detective,* a tightly plotted murder mystery written under the pseudonym Lou Rand, set in a thinly disguised San Francisco at a time when that city was just beginning to consolidate its reputation as the Gay Mecca.

Aday and Maxey changed the name of their business frequently in an effort to avoid run-ins with the police. The ruse wasn't effective, and the two men were constantly

Theodore Sturgeon. *Venus Plus X.* **New York: Pyramid Books, 1960.**
Sturgeon was a self-professed libertine who almost single-handedly brought the mores of the sexual revolution to the field of science fiction. *Venus Plus X* told of a future society in which sexism has been eliminated by the surgical elimination of genital difference and the introduction of artificial reproduction.

Samuel R. Delany. *The Ballad of Beta-2.* **New York: Ace Books, 1965.**
Delany is one of the most accomplished science-fiction authors in America, and *The Ballad of Beta-2* was the first of his many works to be nominated for a major award in the field (Nebula, 1962). It contains minor elements exploring sexual variation, setting the stage for later works like *Dahlgren* and *Triton,* which brought these themes to the fore. *The Motion of Light in Water,* Delany's 1988 memoir, discusses the influences of race and sexuality on his writing.

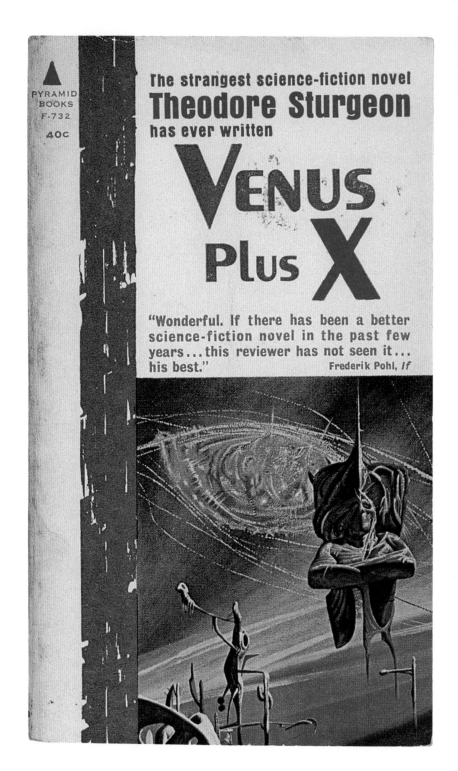

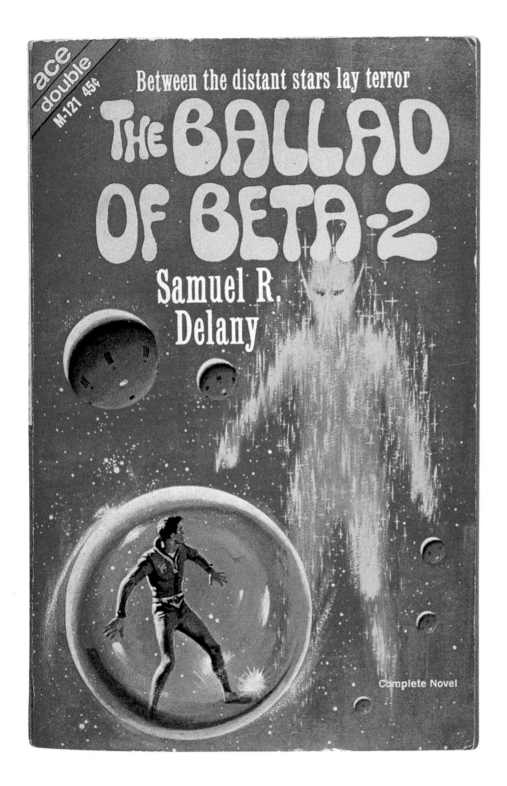

harassed by law enforcement officials intent on shutting down these so-called purveyors of smut. Perhaps in retaliation, they published *Sex Life of a Cop,* which ultimately proved to be their downfall. After sending a copy of that book to a customer in Grand Rapids, Michigan, the two were arrested on federal felony charges for shipping obscene material through the U.S. mail. Their efforts on behalf of freedom of expression made them a cause celebre for a short while in the early 1960s. Their story was championed in early sexual liberation movement publications like *Sex and Censorship,* and drew support from the American Civil Liberties Union. They were nevertheless convicted in 1963, sentenced to twenty-five years in prison, and fined $25,000.

By that late date, however, the golden age of the lurid paperback book was pretty much over, and the sort of punishment meted out to Aday and Maxey for flaunting the sexual mores of a McCarthyite culture would soon be a thing of the past. New Supreme Court rulings significantly narrowed the legal definition of obscenity and broadened the range of permissible public expression. Visual pornography became easier to obtain, undercutting the market for trashy paperbacks. Mainstream movies and books increasingly dealt with themes that had once been relegated to the paperbacks, and the phenomenal success of the paperback format itself had by that time changed the nature of the publishing industry, breaking down many of the old value-laden distinctions between hardcover and paperback works.

The spirit of sexual liberation was in the air by the mid-1960s, and sexual identity movements were soon to follow. Gay, lesbian, bisexual, and transgender people were all beginning to organize politically in the 1960s, and they would transform the social landscape in the decades ahead as they campaigned for their basic human rights. Each of the four remaining chapters in *Queer Pulp* takes as its subject one particular sexual identity group or theme, and follows the trajectory of the paperback books that treated them from the golden age of the late '40s and early '50s through to their tawdry demise in the sleaze books of the 1960s—with allowances being made for a few stray titles of particular interest before or after those years.

Ironically, as queer issues gained the attention and sometimes the sympathy of a larger public audience, queer-themed paperbacks grew less relevant to mainstream American culture. Lesbian PBOs went the way of bouffant hairdos, while gay paperbacks focused increasingly on graphic sexual content in a way that largely limited their appeal to gay men. Bisexual people struggled to define themselves against the "promiscuous swinger" stereotypes that remained rampant in mass-media representations, while transgender people struggled to be seen in literature—when seen at all—as anything other than jokes or freaks or victims of morbid curiosity. Fortunately, by revisiting the paperbacks profiled in this book, we can witness again the tremendous effect of sexual diversity issues on mid-twentieth-century America, and gain a new and deeper appreciation for the roots of an important aspect of our contemporary culture.

Ironically, as queer issues gained the attention and sometimes the sympathy of a larger public audience, queer-themed paperbacks grew less relevant to mainstream American culture.

Bud Clifton. *Muscle Boy.* **New York: Ace Books, 1958.**
"Most men fall in love with women," says the back cover blurb on this trashy novel, "but some men fall in love with themselves!" For naïve teenager Jerry Carpenter, it's a small step from narcissism to exploitation by gay blackmailers who take pictures of beefcake bodybuilders and peddle them to an underground network of perverts. The book fictionalizes a real-life blackmail ring that existed in the San Francisco Bay Area in the 1950s.

Sanford Aday was sentenced to twenty-five years in prison and fined $25,000 in the early 1960s for shipping "dirty books" across state lines. He published dozens of books like those above from the headquarters of his soft-core empire in Fresno, California.

Byron Woolfe. *Bold Desires.*
Fresno, CA: Saber Books, 1959.

Oscar Peck. *Sex Life of a Cop.*
Fresno, CA: Saber Books, 1959.

Eve Linkletter. *The Gay Ones.*
Fresno, CA: Fabian Books, 1958.

Eve Linkletter. *Taxi Dancers.*
Fresno, CA: Fabian Books, 1958.

Twisted Paths and Tangled Webs

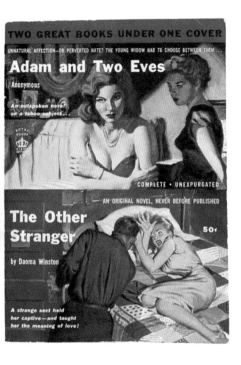

Decades before the proliferation of porn books in the 1960s, bisexuality was depicted in mass-market American paperbacks as a slippery slope leading to any and all deviations from supposed heterosexual norms. By the end of World War II, Freud and his followers had been saying for nearly half a century that every individual was innately bisexual, by which they meant that sexual orientation and gender identity were not fixed at birth but rather took shape and solidified over the course of the childhood years. Potentially, the psychoanalysts claimed, anybody could form an identity as a man or a woman; anybody could fall in love with anybody else; anybody could become aroused by anything whatsoever. It all came down to one's personal history, to the accidental process through which one came to be oneself. In its original form, the theory of innate bisexuality set out to explain the inherent plasticity of human personality, not to advance the claim that every single individual was psychologically wired to enjoy both gay and straight sexual experiences. But in the paranoid style of cold war American popular culture, this Freudian insight became twisted and turned into something sinister—the notion that lurking in the depths of every "normal" man and woman's soul was a raving queer yearning to break free.

The Kinsey reports on male and female sexuality provided ample ammunition for the argument that a broad swath of the American population, at least in terms of their sexual behavior over the course of their lifetime, could, strictly speaking, be characterized as bisexual. In a sense, it would be far more accurate to speak of bisexual pulp literature, rather than gay or lesbian pulps, because there was virtually no discussion of homosexuality in mid-century

Lynton Wright Brent. *Lavender Love Rumble*. **Hollywood, CA: Brentwood Publications, 1965.** Wonderful title, uninspired prose, in this tale of a woman torn between two lovers—a lesbian stripper and a gung-ho Marine.

paperback fiction other than in the context of bisexual love triangles. However, in the paperbacks of that time that explored and exploited Kinsey's revelations, there was little sense of a stable bisexual predisposition. Bisexuality usually served as a first step into a treacherous garden of forking paths, most of which led to homosexuality. The dramatic tension in many of these stories depended not merely on the revelation of bisexuality but rather on the question of how a particular bisexual situation would resolve itself. Perhaps surprisingly, mass market books expressed a variety of opinions regarding that fateful "first step" and depicted a range of possible outcomes for taking it.

Some books that played up the bisexual angle had titles like *The Bitterweed Path* or *The Divided Path,* which reinforced the perception that bisexuality lay at the beginning of a long and uncertain journey. *The Divided Path,* first published in 1949, was reissued in paperback in 1951. The story, which progresses through an escalating series of increasingly taboo encounters, suggests that the division between pornography and erotic realism was perhaps not as clear as wary paperback publishers might like to think. Michael, the main character, begins to stray as a teenager when he fails to suppress that warm feeling he gets when he drapes a protective arm around a young friend. After high school, Michael leaves home to study music. He innocently rents a room at a big-city YMCA, and after only two

weeks he becomes a studied voyeur in the shower rooms. He progresses to massaging a friend's back, during which he feels strong urges he does not understand. Michael then develops a hopeless crush on Paul, the old boyfriend of his high school sweetheart. After that it's on to New York City, the predictable loss of innocence, a torrid threesome, and a "shocking" conclusion—the novel ends on a note of hope that Paul and Michael will find happiness together. The publicity campaign for the hardcover original included an essay contest inviting readers to debate whether the novel's final scene should be altered.

Bisexual plot lines in the postwar decades fell into two broad categories: boy-boy-girl stories and girl-girl-boy stories. The latter type included most of the so-called lesbian pulps, as well a few classic older stories like *Adam and Two Eves,* first published in 1924 and reissued in paperback in 1953. Many of these books were little more than excuses to peddle "lezzie" scenes to none-too-discriminating male readers who wanted reassurance at the story's end that the woman would wind up with the man. One such book was the wonderfully titled (though unfortunately not wonderfully written) *Lavender Love Rumble,* in which our heroine Leslie Dane learns that nothing in this world is really free—not even "free love." Leslie is torn between her mad affair with a famous lesbian striptease artist and an equally passionate fling with a rugged marine sergeant

Dyson Taylor. *Bitter Love.* New York: Pyramid Books, 1957. Alexandra is a pawn in the homosexual affair between her husband, Anton, and his lover, Hugo. She was willing to take the money and status that came with her sham marriage into the Riviera jet set, but now that she's a mother she's determined to get rid of Hugo once and for all and to have Anton all to herself.

Lee Walters. *The Right Bed.* Fresno, CA: Saber Books, 1959. Hmm . . . now which one would that be?

Denys Val Baker. *Strange Fulfillment.* **New York: Pyramid Books, 1958.**
Not every book about a woman with two lovers, one male and the other female, ended in either tragedy or heterosexuality. One of the more visually striking covers produced by Pyramid.

Barry Devlin. *Forbidden Pleasures.* **New York: Berkley Publishing, 1953.**
Triangular love sounds uncomfortable, to say the very least.

Alan Kapelner. *Lonely Boy Blues.* **New York: Lion Books, 1956 (orig. pub.1944).**
"Part story, part heartbeat, part lowdown song, about the guys who pay the price for everything . . . for loving hard and dreaming big . . . but mostly just for living." So says the back cover. Somewhere along the way, one of those guys has a hard-loving homosexual encounter, for which he pays the price.

Ben Travis. *The Strange Ones.* **New York: Universal Publishing and Distribution, 1959.**
The cover says it all in this story of a marriage on the rocks. Wherever the man and woman are looking, it certainly isn't at each other.

Calder Willingham. *End as a Man.* **New York: Avon Publishing, 1952 (orig. pub. 1947).**
Willingham was born in Georgia in 1922 and educated at the Citadel, that bastion of Southern military machismo. The novel is satiric, set at a Southern military institute. The plot revolves around two simpering Leopold- and Loeb-style cadets and one sensitive lost soul. The book was originally condemned as obscene.

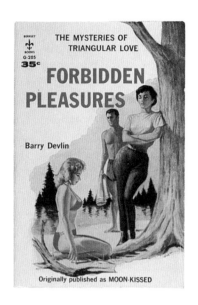

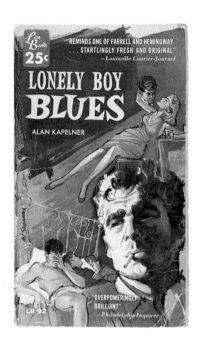

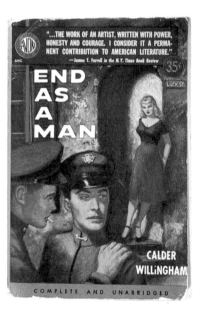

who has ravaged her body and fanned the embers of her soul. She realizes too late that there is a price to pay for the inability to choose between the two sides of her desire—endless days and sleepless nights tormented by her own conscience. Denys Val Baker's *Strange Fulfillment,* on the other hand, suggests that not every love triangle involving two women and a man need end in either tragedy or the triumph of heterosexuality.

Most of the boy-boy-girl triangles, however, did just that. They all implicitly asked the question that *The Right Bed* blatantly stated in its title: Will the male hero wind up in the right bed—that is, the one with the woman in it? Usually the answer was yes—either that, or dead. The blurb on the back cover of Dean Douglas's commendable 1954 paperback original for Fawcett, *Man Divided,* put the question this way: "Could the strength of Sally's love give to him a manhood he had never known, bring him back from the shadows into the sunlight of a wholesome love?" Of course it could. The cover of Richard Meeker's *Torment* asked : "Kurt loved this woman. Did he love her brother more?" Surprisingly, the answer in this case was yes, too. *Torment* was actually a tawdry repackaging of *Better Angel,* one of the earliest gay coming-out novels with a happy ending, published in 1933 under Meeker's real name, Forman Brown. Things did not work out quite so well for the central character in Fritz Peters' *Finistère,* a

sixteen-year-old American in Paris who is rescued from drowning in the Seine, falls in love with his savior and has an affair with him, and then commits suicide because he cannot face his family's rejection.

Finistère illustrates one of the principal frustrations of trying to judge a book by its cover. There is no way to tell, simply by looking at it, that it is a book with a queer theme. Yes, the young man in the foreground looks unhappy about the couple on the couch, but is he jealous for the man's affections, or the woman's? Without reading the story we might never know. Straight folks picking the book up at the corner drugstore might not know they were bringing home a book about a young man's troubled search for his sexual identity, while queer folks looking for a reflection of their own lives in the pages of a paperback book would need to be visually skilled in reading between the lines of deliberately ambiguous images.

The relentless heterosexualization that took place on the covers of many queer books, presumably in an effort to widen their audience, sometimes made it virtually impossible to anticipate the story within. *Lost on Twilight Road,* by James Colton, looks on the surface like a heterosexual romp, but the straight part of the book—if you can call it straight—is dispensed with after the first scene. In this white-trash epic, lonely, sexy sixteen-year-old Lonny is masturbating in his single mom's trailer home one hot

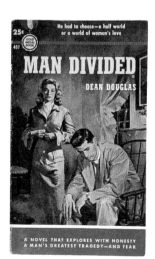

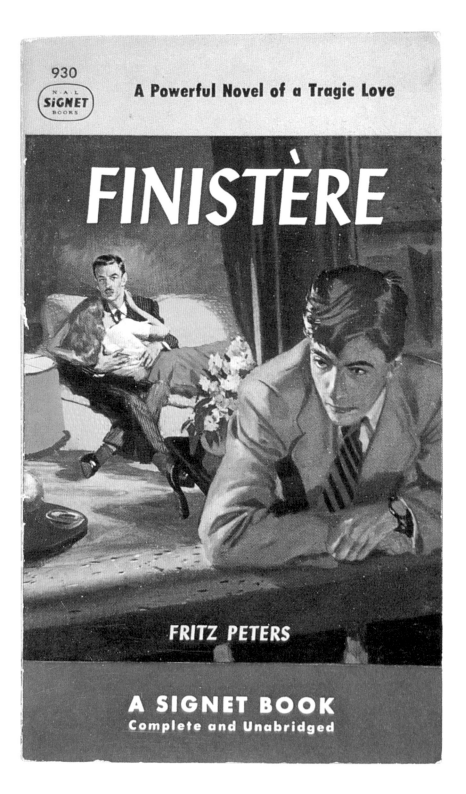

Dean Douglas. *Man Divided.*
New York: Fawcett
Publications, 1954.
From the back cover: "Could the
strength of Sally's love give to him a
manhood he had never known, bring
him back from the shadows into the
sunlight of a wholesome love?" Is that
a rhetorical question, or what?
Douglas himself identified as a gay
man and later wrote several gay porn
books for Greenleaf Classics.

Richard Meeker [Forman
Brown]. *Torment.* **New York:**
Universal Publication and
Distribution, 1951 (orig. pub.
1933 as *Better Angel).*
Not that you'd know by the cover
art, but this was perhaps the first
novel in which the main character finds
happiness when he comes out as gay.

James Colton. *Lost on Twilight*
Road. **Fresno, CA: National**
Library Books, 1964.
Sexy sixteen-year-old Lonny is loafing
in his trailer home one summer after-
noon, when his mother's friend
Mildred drops by with a bottle of
vodka and proceeds to relieve Lonny
of his virginity. The rest of the book is
a gay sex romp.

Fritz Peters [Arthur A. Peters].
Finistère. **New York: Signet**
Books/NAL, 1952.
A sixteen-year-old American in Paris
is saved from drowning by a man with
whom he then has an affair. Unable to
confront his mother with the nature
of his sexuality, he commits suicide.

Louise Sherman. *The Strange Three*. Fresno, CA: Saber Books, 1957.

Bruce Manning. *Triangle of Sin*. New York: Designs Publishing, 1952.

Audry Erskine Lindop. *The Tormented*. New York: Popular Library, 1956.

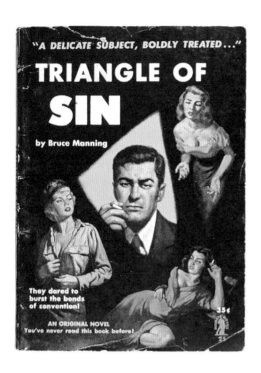

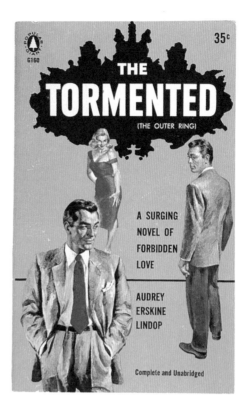

Cover art tells a story in a language all its own.

summer day, when his mother's friend Mildred drops by with a bottle of vodka and proceeds to relieve Lonny of his virginity. He promptly runs away from home, and the rest of the book is a seemingly endless stream of gay sex escapades—not that you'd know it from the cover art.

Cover art on classic paperbacks communicated in a specialized visual vocabulary, employing more of a system in the design and illustrations than might at first be apparent. Consider three bisexual-themed books with similar cover treatments: *Triangle of Sin, The Strange Three,* and *The Tormented.* All use a black and yellow/gold color scheme to produce bold, eye-catching contrasts. At the time these books were printed, however, most publishers avoided using black on paperback covers because it tended to show scratches and wear too easily. It was used primarily on gothic and horror story covers. The extensive use of black on these covers thus subtly suggested the psychological horror a straight mind might experience when confronted with bisexual ménages à trois and the prospect of homosexuality. Note, too, that the black area surrounding the title of the cover of *The Tormented* is a Rorschach inkblot, a further suggestion of psychological torment.

In its placement of human figures, *Triangle of Sin* suggests that the queer relationships are between the women, who occupy the various positions of the triangle, while the man in the center observes all. The cover of *The Tormented,* however, clearly indicates that the queer relationship is between the men. The woman standing in the background, striking a sultry pose in a sexy red dress, goes completely unnoticed by the two men in the foreground, who have eyes only for each other. Notice as well the black line running across the cover, which further separates her from them. *Strange Three* is the least thoughtfully rendered—there are, for example, only two individuals represented—but it is the most slyly amusing: the woman is holding a book titled *Odd Girl,* one of the quintessential lesbian paperbacks.

Lou Morgan's *Hangout for Queers* is not a great book by any conceivable standard. It is not even a very memorable one. The best that can be said of *Hangout for Queers* is that it

perfectly embodies the marginalized genre to which it belongs. Published by Neva Paperbacks of Las Vegas, Nevada, in 1965, it was one of thousands of nondescript volumes that constituted the "adult" book market of the mid-1960s. As with other books of its kind, its length was limited by the publisher for purely economic reasons to approximately sixty-thousand words, which really didn't provide authors with enough room to adequately develop plots and characters, especially since roughly 20 percent of the text of these books was devoted to "hots"—porn industry lingo for the graphic sex scenes. *Hangout for Queers* is, in short, what's crudely known as a fuck book.

As early as 1959, when Ballantine Books published *Pornography and the Law* by doctors Eberhard and Phyllis Kronhausen, the mainstream paperback industry was invested in drawing distinctions between an acceptable work of "erotic realism" and pornography. This was in an effort, no doubt, to dispel the suspicion in some quarters that paperbacks themselves, with their brazen covers and sometimes shocking contents, were inherently immoral. J. W. Erlich, in the introduction to the Kronhausens' book, defined erotic realism as aiming to show the sexual aspects of human personality by depicting internal moods and feelings in a psychologically realistic manner, by representing social situations in which sexual feelings or sexual activity could reasonably be expected to occur, and by exploring the real-life consequences that sexual expression could bring about. The main purpose of pornography, Erlich contended, was simply to stimulate erotic responses in the reader. Pornography accomplished this by presenting a series of scenes depicting erotic wish-fulfillment fantasies arranged from least transgressive to most transgressive, that were capable of creating for the presumably male reader a steadily mounting sense of sexual excitation. According to Erlich's distinction, mass-market paperbacks aimed to provide readers with erotic realism; pornographic books did not.

Pornographic books like *Hangout for Queers* can be distinguished in several other important ways from mass-market paperbacks with queer themes. The mass-market books, published by mainstream presses that offered books

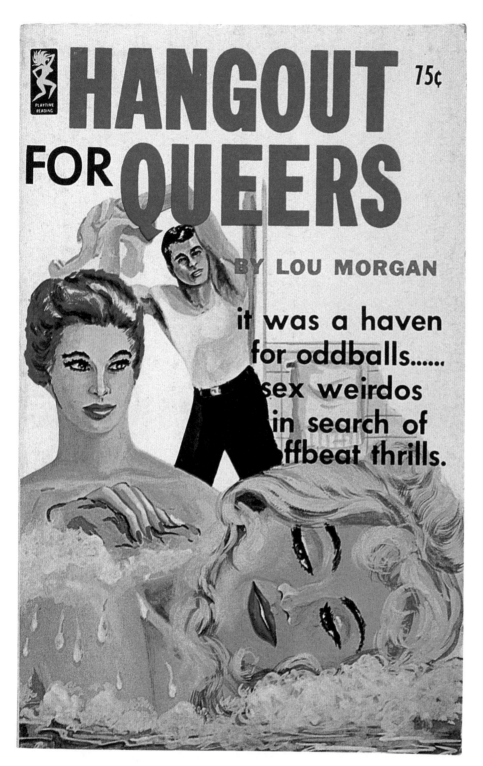

HANGOUT FOR QUEERS

FOR

75¢

BY LOU MORGAN

it was a haven
for oddballs......
sex weirdos
in search of
offbeat thrills.

Lou Morgan. *Hangout for Queers.* Las Vegas, NV: Neva Paperbacks, 1965.
"Queer" in this book means any sexual activity other than heterosexual inter-course for purposes of procreation.

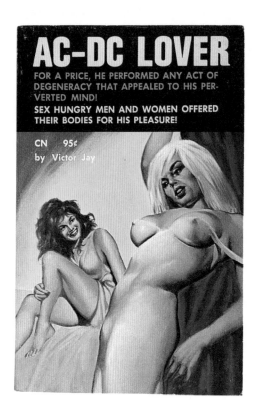
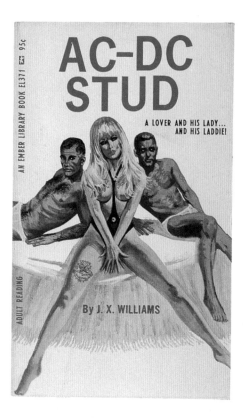

Although little is known about most sleaze paperback writers because of the extensive use of pseudonyms and "house author" names, stylistic similarities suggest that these books were all written by the same person.

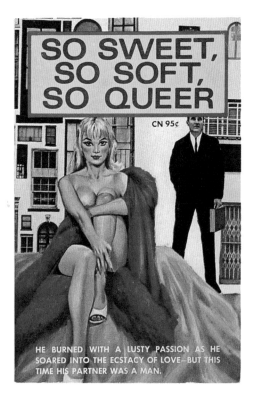

Victor Jay. *AC-DC Lover.*
North Hollywood, CA: Private
Edition Books, 1965.

J. X. Williams. *AC-DC Stud.*
San Diego, CA: Greenleaf
Classics, 1967.

Don Holliday. *The Sin Travellers.*
San Diego, CA: Nightstand
Books, 1962.

Victor Jay. *So Sweet, So Soft, So
Queer.* North Hollywood, CA:
Private Edition, 1965.

Myron Kosloff. *Dial "P" for Pleasure.* **Cleveland, OH: Connoisseur Publications, 1964.** From "A" for algolagnia to "Z" for zoophilia, sleazy paperbacks offered something for every kind of kink.

on a range of topics, generally aimed at reaching a broad audience by exploiting a controversial or sensationalistic topic. Books like *Hangout for Queers* were published by presses that tended to specialize in sexually explicit materials. Rather than trying to reach the broadest possible audience with a particular title, they aimed at catering very narrowly to a single, well-honed erotic need. In this sense these books were not for a mass market but rather for highly specialized ones. Their publishers stayed in business by exploiting as many narrowly defined erotic needs as possible.

Consider, for example, the writing career of Don Holliday, who also published under the names J. X. Williams and Victor Jay, and who worked for several different presses. Under various guises he produced several dozen books in the late 1950s and early 1960s (some of them, admittedly, lifting twenty or thirty pages at a time from previously published work). Holliday wrote some funny and politically pointed gay pulp fiction, like his spy-spoof *The Man from C.A.M.P.,* but he also wrote lesbian novels and swinger novels, plus novels on various other sorts of activities and interests that were simply queer, in the most ecumenical sense of that word. These included *The Sin Travelers* ("They Wanted Kicks—And Didn't Care How They Got Them!"), *AC-DC Lover* ("He Performed Any Act of Degeneracy that Appealed to His Perverted Mind!"), and *So Sweet, So Soft, So Queer* ("He Burned with a Lusty Passion as He Soared into the Ecstasy of Love"). Simply listing the titles of some of his other books gives a pretty good indication of the tenor of Holliday's work: *Blow the Man Down, Flesh Flogger, Hell's Harlot, Lez Lust, Lust Circuit, The Orgy Girls, Passion Pusher, Rally 'Round the Fag, Sex Pack, Shame Doctor, Sin Hotel, The Son Goes Down,* and *Wanton Wife.*

Holliday's presumably gay identity didn't interfere with doing his job, which was to supply a steady stream of new and recycled prose for adult paperbacks that catered to individuals with a broad assortment of tastes—not just to those with a preference for homosexual fantasies. Myron Kosloff's *Dial "P" for Pleasure* similarly suggests the utopian promise of the lurid world depicted in the pages of pornographic paperbacks: it offers an imagined space in which any desire that can be articulated can conceivably be achieved, a place where no request is out of bounds. One could imagine that there it would be just as easy to dial "A" for algolagnia (the enjoyment of pain) or "Z" for zoophilia (enjoying sexual relations with animals), or any other letter in between for whatever one's heart—or loins—desired. Gay, lesbian, bisexual, or transgender themes, in this context, were just a few of the many menu options offered to potential consumers of pornography. In the disreputable fringes of the paperback publishing industry, "queer" was just another niche market waiting to be tapped.

The come-on line plastered across the cover of *Hangout for Queers*—"It was a haven for oddballs—sex weirdos in search of offbeat thrills"— now seems better suited to coaxing a bemused smile from the lips of a vintage paperback collector than it does to inciting curious titillation. Instead of sounding sexy, it sounds almost like something Wally might have said to the Beaver, provoking an indulgent chuckle from Ward and June. But the book's cover blurb indicates something important about the word *queer* itself. *Queer,* in the conceptual universe of mid-twentieth-century lurid paperback books, encompassed a range of erotic expression that had nothing to do with homosexuality per se. It could refer to any sexual act other than missionary-position attempts at procreation.

In the hands of underpaid or ignorant hacks, the dazzling, potentially bewildering varieties of "queer" desire could collapse into one undifferentiated puddle—often with hilarious results. The cover art for *Abnormals Anonymous* was apparently created by someone who had only the most rudimentary sense of sexual minority experience. It is a complete hodgepodge of elements, each piled haphazardly on top of the next, each individually intending to signify "queerness" in some generic sense but together not forming a coherent whole. We see a short-haired woman in the foreground, wearing pants and smoking a cigar. A man in a skirt sits knitting in a chair, his legs demurely crossed, as another woman looks down at him. There is no "erotic realism" rooted in society or history or sexual practice to hold the scene together. It is nothing more than a crude rendition

by STELLA GRAY | Never had so desperate a group of human beings banded together . . . ABNORMALS ANONYMOUS.

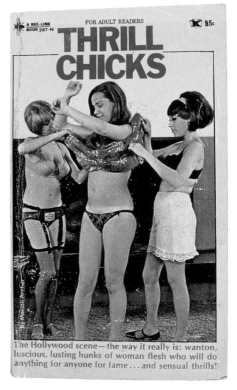

Stella Gray. *Abnormals Anonymous.* **Fresno, CA: National Library Books, 1964.** National Library Books was on the lower end of the paperback publishing spectrum, and it shows in the cover design of *Abnormals Anonymous,* a mishmash of cross-wired gender signifiers that suggests little more than the artist's confusion about her subject matter.

Marion Archer. *Thrill Chicks.* **New York: Bee-Line Books, 1969.** The sexual revolution of the later 1960s gave the moribund juvenile delinquent genre a new lease on life in this quickie exploitation effort.

WOMEN LUSTED AFTER THIS HANDSOME, VIRILE JAZZMAN ... IT TOOK HIM YEARS OF AGONY TO REALIZE HE WANTED A MAN

HOT PANTS HOMO

By PERCY FENSTER

95c CN

BISEXUAL ... HE TOOK ON MALE AND FEMALE ALIKE

Percy Fenster. *Hot Pants Homo.* **North Hollywood, CA: All Star Books, 1964.**
Wayne, a ruggedly handsome jazz musician, is seduced by a beautiful blonde woman in the opening chapter of *Hot Pants Homo,* but he can't consummate his passion because, in the memorable words of author Percy Fenster, "Wayne is a faggot, a queer, a homosexual." After many bisexual escapades in which he tries to determine his true sexual identity, Wayne finally finds a woman psychiatrist who sets him straight. An inscrutably confusing cover treatment for an inscrutably confused book.

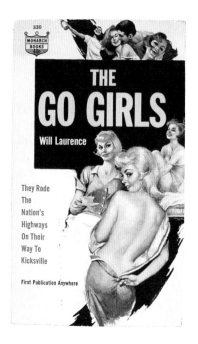

of an ill-defined fantasy. That naïve simplicity is undoubtedly the source of whatever appeal the book may have achieved in the eyes of collectors and connoisseurs of mid-twentieth-century American popular culture.

Hot Pants Homo is similarly muddled. In spite of the word *homo* splashed in big red letters across the front cover, we see a man and woman in a passionate heterosexual embrace. The "homo" is then identified as a bisexual who takes on "men and women alike." Another blurb tells us that although women lust after the handsome Wayne, he realizes after years of agony that he wants to be with a man. The story ends, however, with a the guilt-ridden, psychologically tortured protagonist seeking the services of a woman psychiatrist who restores his heterosexuality and marries him. The target market for both this book and *Abnormals Anonymous* seems to have been people for whom homosexuality played some role in their sexual fantasies, but who were so poorly informed about the actual practice that they could imagine it only indistinctly, as part of some alternative queer space lying somewhere beyond the pale of normalcy.

Like everything else about the paperback phenomenon, bisexual themes changed over time. In the 1940s and '50s they provided an avenue for approaching the question of homosexuality. By the later 1960s, they were just another flavor of porn. In between those periods, bisexuality played a role in two other paperback genres, both related to changes in American culture in the late 1950s and early 1960s: juvenile delinquent stories and swinger fiction.

The juvenile delinquent genre so popular in that period often made use of bisexual themes. Sexual experi-mentation is a normal part of adolescence, but in an era when teenagers were beginning to be portrayed in the media as rebels without a cause, it was only natural that experimentation with taboo forms of sexuality would figure in stories about kids gone bad. In Will Laurence's *The Go Girls,* for example, Margo Thaxton and Dot Martin ride with the Wildcats, a tough gang of cycle-straddling vixens who grab life by the throat and shake it until they get what they want. Margo is presented as a confirmed "diesel dyke," while Dot is described as an "ambisextrous" wench who reaches for her switchblade at the slightest insult, real or imagined. As the cover says, they're on "the highway to Kicksville," where erotic pleasures await in a variety of fleshly forms.

Once the swinger scene started in the early 1960s, bisexuality became fashionable not just for youth but for older folks, too. In many ways this development represented the other side of the situation created by the "innate bisexuality" argument. In the swinger ethos everybody was bisexual, just like Freud said, but this was considered a good thing rather than a tragedy. In the early days of the sexual revolution, even married people living in the suburbs could be queer if they could just get over their hang-ups and repressions.

One of the most influential books to exploit the subject of swinging was *The Velvet Underground,* by Florida newspaper correspondent Michael Leigh, published by McFadden in 1963. Leigh's exposé of wife-swapping swingers in the suburbs of America deplores the sexual depravity of the modern age, but goes into detailed descriptions of sexual subcultures that make you wonder how the author gained his wealth of knowledge. According to the

Will Laurence. *The Go Girls.* Darby, CT: Monarch Books, 1963. Margo Thaxton and Dot Martin ride with the Wildcats, a tough gang of cycle-straddling vixens who grab life by the throat and shake it until they get what they want. Margo's an out-and-out diesel dyke. Dot's an "ambisextrous" wench who reaches for her switchblade at the slightest insult, real or imagined. They're looking for kicks, kicks, and more kicks—pity the poor man who stands in their way!

Martin Mansfield. *Odd Couple.* Las Vegas, NV: Neva Paperbacks, 1967. A routine "swinger" paperback.

Bob Blake. *Gay Gay a Go-Go.* Aquora, CA: PAD Library, 1966. Note the discrepancy between the cover art and the title—a fine example of the relentless heterosexualization of paperback art.

Marcus Miller. *The Flesh Happening.* San Diego, CA: Phenix Publishers, 1967. Hippies and Harlots and Sin Scenes—Oh, My! Marcus Miller was another of those prolific paperback writers who produced prose for whatever genre and whatever publisher needed a new title at the moment.

Fortunately, the sexual revolution of the 1960s was only beginning . . .

author himself, Leigh noticed an ad in a magazine he found in a hotel lobby. The ad announced the formation of a "new and unusual friendship club," one in which members could "exchange strange experiences and discuss the bizarre and exotic." Leigh thought it was a club for world travelers like himself. He answered the ad, thinking he would be comparing notes with other Americans on the quirks of quaint people living in countries with unpronounceable names, little realizing he was heading into a "velvet underground" of wife-swappers, corset-lovers, orgy-goers, and garden-variety bisexuals, gays, lesbians, and transvestites.

The Velvet Underground would be a fun read, with a few interesting historical nuggets on the early sexual liberation subculture thrown in for good measure, if not for the insidious moralizing wrapped around Leigh's wide-eyed exposé. The book contains an introduction by one Louis Berg, M.D., identified on the flyleaf as "a professional lecturer on topics of psychological interest" who has "studied abroad." He undoubtedly has many other equally impressive "qualifications." Anxious to shore up the crumbling façade of normative heterosexuality that he fears is collapsing around him, Berg spews some of the most hateful, perversely twisted antiqueer propaganda ever printed in a mainstream American paperback book. It is a stunning example of the hysterical mindset that considers any deviation from the norm to be the first step on the pathway to ultimate perversion.

Homosexuals and transgender people represent the absolute nadir of humankind, in Berg's opinion, and yet they have somehow gained special privileges:

In America, as in Europe, they have their own bars and clubs, their restaurants, their magazines and newsletters. They even have certain areas of the city where they can flaunt themselves without interference. But this is not enough. This ilk is never content to remain prisoners of

their own abnormality. It would seem to be a condition of their aberrant drives that, as some light-skinned Negroes, they should "pass." And it is here that they frequently come into open conflict with the law. For it is as at such times that they attempt to raid the ranks of the normal.

Crossing social boundaries of any kind is likely, from Berg's point of view, to bring about the end of civilization. But even his racist paranoia pales in comparison to his assertion that members of the "velvet underground" in Berlin helped bring Hitler to power. Berg says of his visit to Berlin just before World War II:

I visited the night locales where Lesbians flaunted their warped love; I danced with transvestites and did not know I was doing so until I was informed by my conductor; I sat at tables in special bars where old men preened and postured and paraded their young paramours. One café was devoted solely to a clientele of flagellants. . . . Scattered throughout the country, nudist camps and locales for sundry forms of abnormal nature worship did not bother to conceal or mask the saturnalia of sex. Indeed, the Germany of Adolf Hitler would have been the paradise of many who are described in The Velvet Underground.

Berg seems to have forgotten somehow that the people he described in prewar Berlin would most likely have been sent to the concentration camps , but no matter—that doesn't fit with his conspiracy theory about how nice, normal heterosexual people are being seduced into immoral pastimes by queer people who pass as straight, thus inevitably leading the nation down the path to fascist domination.

Fortunately, the sexual revolution of the 1960s was only beginning, and reactionary voices like Berg's were soon drowned out in the excitement of the new moral climate.

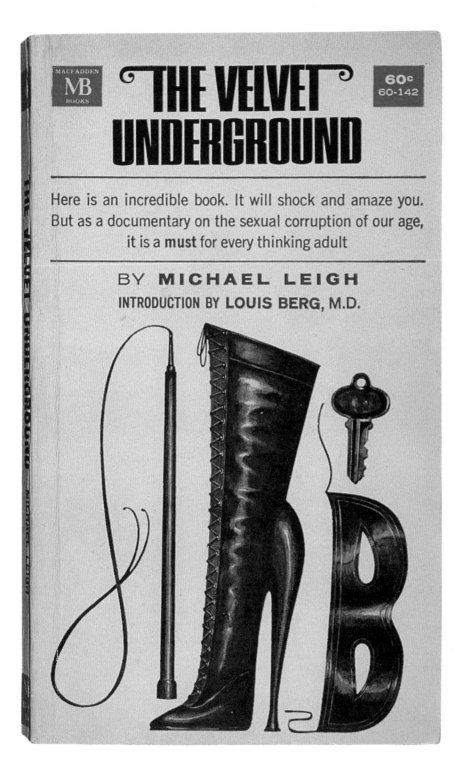

Michael Leigh. *The Velvet Underground.* **New York: McFadden Books, 1963.** This exposé of wife-swapping swingers in the suburbs of America deplores the sexual depravity of the modern age. Homosexuality is deplored most of all, but sadism, masochism, and promiscuity are all closely tied for second place.

Lesbian Lives and Lusts

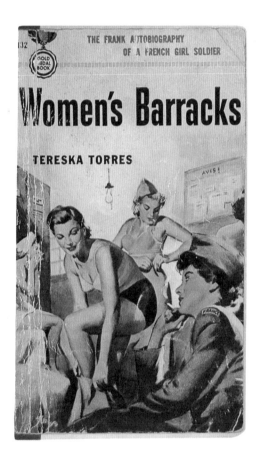

Tereska Torres. *Women's Barracks.* Greenwich, CT: Fawcett Publications, 1950.
The first lesbian paperback original. In spite of her marriage to journalist and screenwriter Meyer Levin, Torres wrote several other lesbian novels in the late '50s and early '60s, including *The Golden Cage, The Only Reason,* and *By Cecile.*

Tereska Torres didn't intend to launch the golden age of lesbian paperback originals with her autobiographically based novel *Women's Barracks,* published by Fawcett in 1950—but that is precisely what she did. Born in Paris in 1921, Torres was the daughter of highly regarded Beaux Arts sculptor Marek Swarc and his wife Guida, Polish Jews who had converted to Catholicism and taken up residence in France in the early 1900s. Barely eighteen years old when the war against Hitler broke out, Torres joined Charles de Gaulle's Free French Army in 1939 and spent most of the war in London working in the resistance movement. After her first husband was killed in combat, Torres married American war journalist Meyer Levin, whose searing eyewitness accounts of the liberation of the concentration camps helped shape initial public awareness of the Holocaust. Torres introduced her second husband to the early French edition of Anne Frank's diary, and he introduced the diary to American readers through a front-page story in the *New York Times.* Both Torres and Levin were involved in the eventual publication of Frank's diary in English, as well as its dramatization on stage and screen.

Women's Barracks was drawn from Torres's experiences in London during World War II, and it was not written with a specifically lesbian audience in mind. Rather, it was intended more broadly as a novel about women in wartime. Although it dealt in a frank and straightforward manner with the fact that some women under those circumstances were sexually active with other women, this was not its principal concern. One thread of the plot involves Ursala, a young woman of seventeen who falls in love with a coarse but maternal older bisexual woman

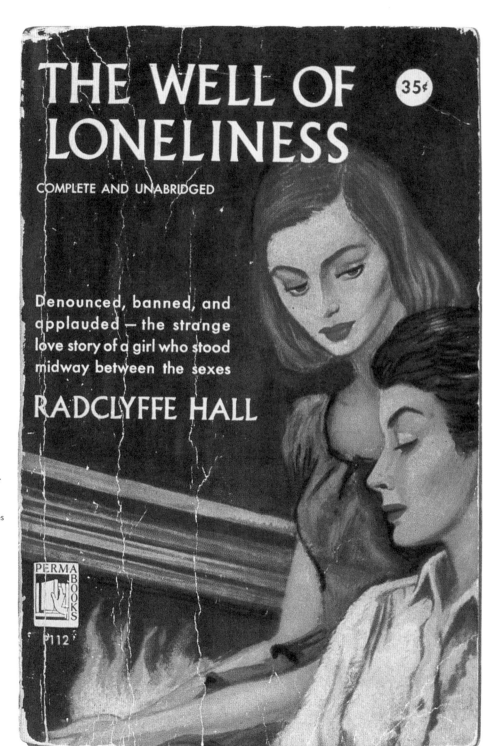

Radclyffe Hall. *The Well of Loneliness.* **New York: Perma Books, 1951.**
Probably the most famous lesbian novel of the twentieth century, originally published in 1928. Author Radclyffe Hall was friends with the English sexologist Havelock Ellis, whose famous theory of "sexual inversion" was reflected in the pages of her book.

named Claude, who has entered into a marriage of convenience with a self-professed "pansy." Some exclusively lesbian couples involved with the Free French Army look down upon Ursala and Claude as promiscuous perverts, but the relationship proves to be a good one for the younger woman, who uses it to gain a better sense of herself before returning to relationships with men, presumably from a position of greater maturity and self-awareness.

Torres's book struck a cord with readers of every gender and sexual orientation, selling over a million copies in 1950. It had been reprinted thirteen times by 1964 and sold over three million copies before it finally went out of print. By 1952 the book had achieved enough notoriety to be singled out for condemnation by the Gathings Committee, a politically reactionary congressional investigation into the supposedly subversive influences of paperbacks. Although members of the committee had read *Women's Barracks,* they refused to quote it in their *Report of the Select Committee into Current Pornographic Materials,* claiming that its lesbian passages—which were actually quite restrained—were too graphic to be included in a government document. The report created a climate of fear in the publishing industry by threatening fines and jail terms for those who refused to embrace the Committee's vision of morality. This resulted in a general toning-down of sexual content in paperbacks, particularly in their cover art, and in a greater emphasis on stories that drove home the generally tragic consequences of straying from a straight and narrow path.

In its condemnation of *Women's Barracks,* the Gathings Committee was also reacting to the previous history of lesbian-themed paperbacks. Mass-market paperbacks had contained lesbian content since the early days of the "paperback revolution" launched by Pocket Books in 1939. Most publishers of these earlier lesbian titles had coyly justified their attention to the potentially sensationalistic topic by presenting it in the form of reprinted historical fiction, usually by European authors. Emile Zola's *Nana* (originally published in 1880) was a particular favorite. Pocket Books, the most straight-laced and family-oriented of all the paperback publishing houses, created a stir with its 1941 edition, the racy cover of which showed the brazen heroine in a revealing, diaphanous white gown. Despite public protests, *Nana* was reprinted twelve times and became one of the most popular titles issued to troops in special armed services editions during World War II. The short-lived, Chicago-based Quick Reader company published its own edition of *Nana* in 1945, and Pocket Books repeated its earlier success in 1947 with another edition featuring an even more scandalously attired title character on the cover. Pocket Books defended itself against charges of crass exploitation by insisting that the sexy *Nana* covers were not gratuitous and were in fact intrinsically related to the themes of this classic literary work.

By situating homosexuality "over there" in decadent Europe, and by safely relegating it to an earlier historical period, American paperback publishers apparently

The report created a climate of fear in the publishing industry by threatening fines and jail terms for those who refused to embrace the Committee's vision of morality.

hoped to make the topic palatable enough for domestic consumption without surrendering the opportunity to cash in on the public's anxious fascination with queer stories. Quick Reader offered American audiences another nineteenth-century French novel with lesbian content in its 1945 reprint of Theophile Gautier's *Mademoiselle de Maupin,* first published in 1835. Daphne du Maurier's 1938 historical romance, *Rebecca,* was published by Pocket Books in 1943. According to Laurence Miller's bibliography of golden age gay and lesbian paperbacks, only three paperback reprints in the 1940s relied on more contemporary settings for their lesbian stories. These were Dorothy Baker's *Trio* (Penguin, 1946; originally published in 1943); Mary Renault's *Promise of Love* (Dell, 1949; originally published in 1939), and Felice Swados's *Reform School Girl* (Diversey Romance Novel, 1949; originally published in 1941 as *House of Fury*), now one of the titles most sought after by vintage paperback collectors.

The pace of lesbian paperback publishing picked up in 1950. In addition to Tereska Torres's *Women's Barracks,* three lesbian-themed reprints also appeared that year: *Imperial City,* by Elmer Rice (Avon, originally published in 1937); *Halo in Brass,* an early lesbian/detective story by John Evans (Pocket Books, originally published in 1949) in which an elderly couple hires a private eye to learn the whereabouts of their missing daughter; and James Ronald's saga of life behind bars, *The Angry Woman* (Bantam, originally published in 1948). Perhaps the most famous lesbian novel of all, Radclyffe Hall's 1928 *Well of Loneliness,* was reprinted by Perma Books in 1951. The story of Stephen Gordon, a wretched "invert" who loves women and feels like a masculine soul trapped in a female body, had been banned in England but became a best-seller everywhere else. Its

paperback publication rekindled all the old debates about the book's supposed obscenity, generating sales of over one hundred thousand copies in 1951, and paving the way for another handful of lesbian novels to appear as mass-market paperbacks.

Also in 1951, Avon offered yet another nineteenth-century French potboiler, Alphonse Daudet's 1884 *Sappho,* as well as Lilyan Brock's 1935 *Queer Patterns.* This overwrought tale involves a musical-comedy star, married to a perfect husband, whose true talent for serious drama shines only under the knowing direction of a strong-willed woman. A home-wrecking lesbian affair ensues, but the women must part or face professional ruin. The remainder of the book is a veritable descent into hell: there is a long illness brought about by the heartbreak of separation, a bad remarriage, and a jealousy-inspired suicide. The star ultimately dies at the hand of her violent, drug-addicted second husband. Another book reprinted that year, Lucie Marchal's *The Mesh* (Bantam; originally published in English in 1949), was of considerably higher literary quality. The psychologically complex story treats the effects of a domineering woman's personality on her grown son and daughter. The son repudiates his mother's style of womanhood by marrying a brow-beaten young widow, who then becomes the object of the daughter's sympathy. The two women eventually become romantically involved, but the daughter is inexorably drawn into acting out the same emotional tyrannies that she despises in her own mother, thus perpetuating the cycle of domination and rebellion that she had hoped to escape.

The best lesbian reprint of 1951, however, was Gale Wilhelm's *We Too Are Drifting* (Lion, originally published in 1935). Wilhelm wrote in the lean, economical style

Lilyan Brock. *Queer Patterns.* New York: Eton (Avon), 1952. Originally published in 1935, this overwrought melodrama involves the ill-fated romance between an actor and her director.

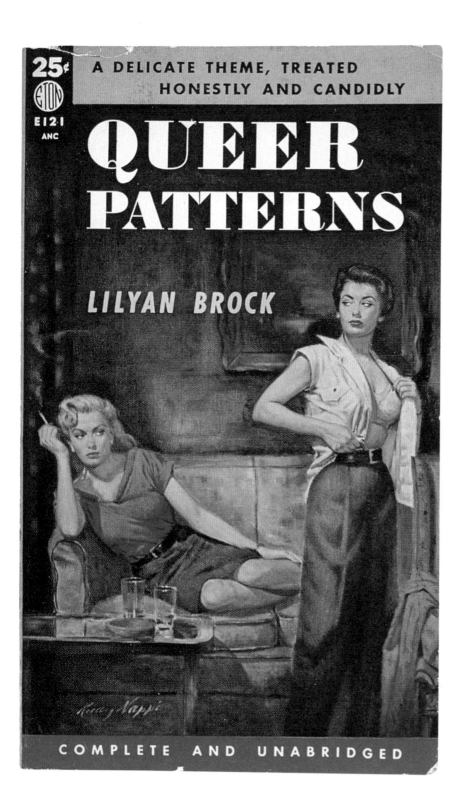

Gale Wilhelm. *We Too Are Drifting.* **New York: Berkley Books, 1955 (orig. pub. 1935).** One of the better lesbian novels by a serious—and seriously under-valued—woman writer. Wilhelm also wrote the equally meritorious *Torchlight to Valhalla* in 1938, which was published in paperback as *The Strange Path* by Lion in 1953.

The new trend in paperback originals created a huge market for the work of competent women writers,

several of them lesbians, who might otherwise never have gotten their works into print at the established hardcover publishing houses.

popularized by Ernest Hemingway; according to Jeannette Foster's pathbreaking critical survey, *Sex-Variant Women in Literature,* the "grudging acclaim" Wilhelm's debut novel received "would certainly have been warmer and more voluminous except for her subject." *We Too Are Drifting* treats the life and loves of Jan Morale, an androgynous young woodcut artist who serves as the model for her mentor's prize-winning sculpture, Hermaphroditus. The sculptor would like to marry Jan, but he recognizes she is unavailable to any man. She is in fact involved, in Foster's wonderful turn of phrase, "with a society beauty who has raised marital deception to a fine art in the interests of her predatory lesbian habits." However, Jan soon falls in love with Victoria, a recent college graduate and only child who lives with her doting parents in their comfortable suburban home. The unfolding romance between the two women, as well as the tensions in their relationship, is presented with considerable realism and sophistication. Eventually the differences in their backgrounds and expectations of life prove too great for the couple, and the reader is left alone with the despondent Jan Morale, watching as Victoria sets off on a cross-country trip with her parents and the nice young man they hope for her to marry.

In 1952, Fawcett Books was flush with the unprecedented success of *Women's Barracks.* They were undoubtedly aware of the surge in lesbian paperback reprints and the impressive sales figures other publishers were racking up with them, yet mindful of the repressive political climate that had settled over the nation. They thus set out to incorporate lesbian-oriented material into their new Gold Medal series of paperback originals. Their new emphasis on paperback originals had emerged from a loophole recently discovered in Fawcett's distribution contract with Signet, which forbid the former company—at that point a publisher of magazines as well as hardcover books—from entering the lucrative paperback reprint market. The contract did, however, allow Fawcett to publish original material in any format. They promptly took advantage of this previously unrealized opportunity by offering unknown authors cash advances of several thousand dollars to write new novels for the paperback trade.

The market in paperback originals gave Fawcett the ability to dictate a new novel's content in ways that had been impossible with reprint titles, thus conveniently helping to ensure that the new books met right-wing standards of political correctness even while they exploited controversial subjects. Left-leaning playwright Lillian Hellman made headlines in 1952 when she defiantly told the House Un-American Activities Committee, "I cannot and will not cut my conscience to fit this year's fashions," but many other unconventional women felt they didn't have the luxury of high-profile resistance to the dominant culture. The new trend in paperback originals created a huge market for the work of competent women writers, several of them lesbians, who might otherwise never have gotten their works into print at the established hardcover publishing houses. For those willing to work within the restrictive conventions of the new genre, lesbian-oriented paperback originals allowed a significant number of

S774

GOLD MEDAL BOOK

35¢

Of the love that dwells in twilight
—the "love that can never be told"

WE WALK ALONE
Through Lesbos' Lonely Groves

ANN ALDRICH

Ann Aldrich [Marijane Meaker].
We Walk Alone. **Greenwich, CT: Fawcett Publications, 1955.**
In 1952, under the name Vin Packer, Marijane Meaker wrote *Spring Fire*, one of the most successful of Fawcett's lesbian paperback originals. She also wrote lesbian fiction as Ann Aldrich, and later had an award-winning career as the author of juvenile fiction, using the name M. E. Kerr.

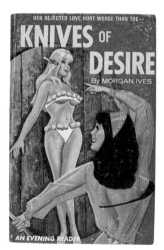

Morgan Ives [Marion Zimmer Bradley]. *Knives of Desire.* **San Diego, CA: Corinth Publications, 1966.**
One of Marion Zimmer Bradley's trashier titles. It involves a young woman who joins the circus and, in need of a protector, takes up with the lesbian knife thrower. Little does our heroine know that the new friend for whom she agrees to become a human target is prone to murderous outbursts of jealous rage. Bradley also wrote under the names Miriam Gardner and Lee Chapman.

women a somewhat subversive opportunity to represent contemporary lesbian life with an unprecedented degree of sympathy and realism.

Vin Packer's 1952 *Spring Fire* was Fawcett's first lesbian paperback specifically designed to capitalize on the success of *Women's Barracks*. Packer was a pseudonym for real-life lesbian Marijane Meaker, who also wrote under the name Ann Aldrich and later went on to great success as award-winning juvenile fiction author M. E. Kerr. In an interview described by Lee Server in his history of lurid paperbacks, *Over My Dead Body,* Meaker claimed that *Spring Fire* was the result of a chance conversation with Fawcett editor Dick Caroll. She had just written an article on girls' boarding schools for the *Ladies' Home Journal,* and when Caroll asked if there was any lesbian activity at boarding schools, Meaker assured him that there was— and a lot more of it in colleges. Caroll then told her about the new line of Fawcett paperback originals and asked her to write a lesbian story for them. "The only restriction he gave me," Meaker recalled, "was that it couldn't have a happy ending." Otherwise, she claimed, "the Post Office might seize the books as obscene."

Spring Fire recounts the ill-fated romance of Leda and Mitch, two Tri Epsilon sorority sisters at Cranston University, a small liberal arts college in the Midwest. Boyish Mitch is the naïve newcomer, Leda the popular, jaded, and seductive upper-class woman with whom Mitch shares a room. Leda is a guilt-ridden neurotic who sleeps around with women as well as men, and she cautions Mitch not to become too attached to her. Bisexual promiscuity can be chalked up to youthful indiscretion, Leda explains,

but exclusive homosexuality will bring down the wrath of the authorities. Mitch will hear none of it, convinced that Leda is her one true love. Slowly, Leda comes around and falls in love with Mitch. Then, just as the editor ordered, the book ends on a tragic note. The haughty Leda can't cope with the loss of status that comes with being labeled a lesbian once her affair with Mitch comes to light. She breaks down under all the social pressure, becomes psychotic, and winds up committed to an insane asylum.

Spring Fire was one of the best-selling novels of 1952. In spite of the obligatory downbeat ending, it managed to represent lesbianism as a more or less unremarkable aspect of some college women's campus life, and to at least hint at the possibility that, however badly it worked out this time, a healthy lesbian relationship was not entirely unthinkable. Mitch is a sympathetic character, and Leda is portrayed as a pathetic victim of intolerance rather than as an evil villainess. *Spring Fire* called attention to an enthusiastic lesbian readership whose extent had not been appreciated previously, but one to which Fawcett and other mainstream paperback publishers would cater for the next fifteen years. Meaker received hundreds of letters from lesbians throughout the United States, pleading for more books like *Spring Fire* with a semblance of realistic contemporary lesbian content. Although "Vin Packer" went on to write male-oriented crime and juvenile delinquent fiction, Meaker developed "Ann Aldrich" as her lesbian literary mouthpiece. The novels she wrote under that name, including *We Walk Alone, We Too Must Love,* and *We Two Won't Last* earned her an avid following among lesbians.

Marion Zimmer Bradley and the Friends of Darkover. *Free Amazons of Darkover.* **New York: Daw Books, 1985.**
Though she's better known for science fiction and fantasy novels like *The Mists of Avalon,* Marion Zimmer Bradley wrote several lesbian paperbacks under various pseudonyms. *Free Amazons of Darkover,* though published considerably after the golden age of lesbian paperback books, brings together both of her longstanding interests.

Meaker's Ann Aldrich novels were earnestly discussed in the pages of the *Ladder*, the pioneering lesbian periodical published by the first lesbian civil rights organization, the Daughters of Bilitis, founded in 1956. Barbara Grier, who later established lesbian-focused Naiad Press, regularly reviewed lesbian paperbacks for the *Ladder*, using the pseudonym Gene Damon. Grier and her fellow *Ladder* contributor Marion Zimmer Bradley, who penned a number of lesbian paperbacks herself before winning fame for her fantasy and science-fiction tales, compiled the first annotated bibliographies of lesbian paperbacks based on their *Ladder* reviews. Their astute observations reveal the careful attention many mid-twentieth-century lesbian readers paid to lesbian-themed mass-market paperbacks, their hunger for affirming representations, their ability to tease out subtextual sympathies in books that were often overtly homophobic and misogynistic, and their loyal appreciation for authors who expressed carefully coded support for the kind of lives they led.

A generation of lesbian writers who worked within the formulaic constraints of the lesbian paperback genre took shape between the early 1950s and the mid-1960s. Probably the most famous of these was Patricia Highsmith, later renowned for writing *The Talented Mr. Ripley* and other suspense novels. Using the name Claire Morgan, in 1952 she wrote *The Price of Salt*, in which the young orphan Therese sets out for an acting career in New York City, but settles instead for a job in the toy department of a large department store, where she meets wealthy regular customer Carol.

After a few doll sales and come-hither looks, the two women retreat happily ever after to Carol's country house. *The Price of Salt* has the reputation of being the first lesbian novel to end on an upbeat note. A paperback version appeared in 1953, and eventually sold more than a million copies.

One of the more prolific lesbian authors was Valerie Taylor, who had been born Velma Young in Aurora, Illinois, in 1913. Taylor published her first lesbian paperback, *Whisper Their Love*, in 1957, followed by *Stranger on Lesbos, Return to Lesbos, A World Without Men, Unlike Others, Journey to Fulfillment*, and her greatest commercial success, *The Girls in 3-B*, a censored version of which became a long-running syndicated comic strip. Taylor took an active part in the gay liberation and lesbian feminist movements that emerged in the 1960s and '70s, acquiring the nickname "everybody's favorite lesbian grandmother." As a practicing Quaker, she had a longstanding commitment to social justice work and was involved in the antinuclear movement as well as the Gray Panthers.

Taylor's happy success in life contrasts sharply with the sad fate of Sloane Britain, another prolific lesbian paperback writer whose career was chronicled by Barbara Grier and Marion Zimmer Bradley in their annual checklists of lesbian literature for the *Ladder*. They described Britain's 1959 debut effort, *First Person . . . 3rd Sex*, as a "well-written novel of a young schoolteacher" who comes, "through bitter experience, to accept her own lesbian nature." They rated it as "one of the best paperback novels," deserving of better presentation than it received.

Claire Morgan [Patricia Highsmith]. *The Price of Salt.* **New York: Bantam,1953.**
Patricia Highsmith was a native of Fort Worth, Texas, but spent most of her career living in Europe. She wrote the novel upon which Alfred Hitchcock's classic thriller *Strangers on a Train* was based, and also worked on the screenplay. Highsmith created a macabre antihero in *The Talented Mr. Ripley.* Before those achievements, however, Highsmith wrote *The Price of Salt,* widely regarded as the first lesbian paperback to have a happy ending.

Valerie Taylor. *Unlike Others.* **New York: Tower Publications, 1963.**
Taylor was a real-life lesbian who had an active career in lesbian-feminist politics and culture in the 1970s and 1980s. She donated her literary manuscripts and other papers to Cornell University.

Sloane Britain. *First Person, 3rd Sex.* **Chicago: Newsstand Library, 1959.**
Sloane Britain wrote a number of cynical, soul-searching lesbian paperback originals before taking her own life in 1964. She was apparently depressed at being unable to escape from hack writing and to express her true talent as an author.

W. D. Sprague, Ph.D. *The Lesbian in Our Society.* **New York: Midwood Tower Publications, 1962.**
Unlike most pseudo-scientific mass-marketed "studies" of sexual diversity, Sprague's book on lesbians was surprisingly unbiased.

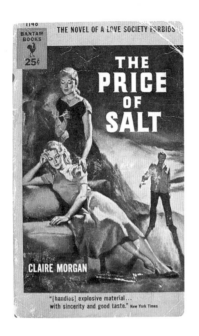

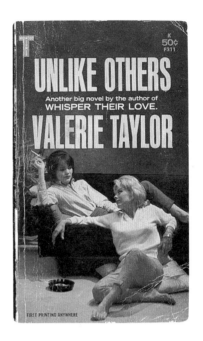

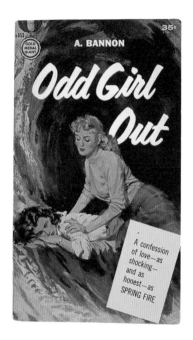

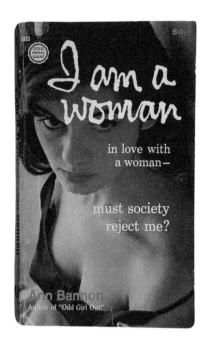

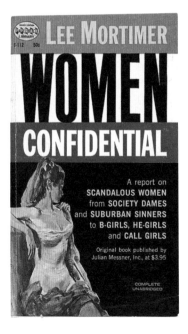

However, they considered Britain's *The Needle,* also published in 1959, to be a "contrived shocker" about "a young girl who falls simultaneously into lesbianism, drug addiction, prostitution, and the hands of a couple dabbling in incest." Although "better written that the average evening waster," they continued, it "leaves a bitter taste." They thought *Meet Marilyn* (1960) included a "good portrait of a well-integrated lesbian household" and recommended *These Curious Pleasures* (1961), a purported autobiography, for its excellent writing and characterization. They condemned *Woman Doctor* (1962), a novel about "a mixed-up woman psychiatrist seducing her own patients," as being "far below the original standard which the early works of this author led us to expect." *Insatiable* (1963) they dismissed as "well-written trash, illustrating perfectly the plight of the competent writer who must write paperback originals for mass tastes, or stop writing altogether." A final note appended to one of their later checklists remarked, "Sloane M. Britain died, by her own hand, in her New York apartment in early 1964. In spite of the gradually declining and cynical character of her later books, we feel that the literary world has lost a promising talent. She might well have escaped the rut of hackwork, and written something well worthwhile. We'll never know."

Of all the lesbian paperback writers from the pre-1965 golden age, Ann Bannon (a pseudonym for Sacramento-based writer Ann Thayer) has enjoyed the greatest longevity and achieved the greatest critical success. Her six-volume series featuring Greenwich Village bar butch Beebo Brinker and friends Laura, Beth, and Jack was originally published between 1957 and 1962. Unlike many of the more exploitative lesbian paperbacks, Bannon's stories have fully realized characters who develop over time, credible and well-crafted plots, and emotional complexity as well as some steamy sex scenes. They have become part of both lesbian and feminist literary canons and have been reissued in numerous subsequent editions. Other notable lesbian PBO authors include March Hastings, Paula Christian, Rea Michaels, Randy Salem, and Artemis Smith. Altogether, at least fifteen lesbian authors during the golden age produced over a hundred paperbacks in which lesbianism was presented in as favorable a light as publishers would allow.

Paperbacks with reasonably sympathetic stories actually written by lesbian authors constituted only a tiny fraction of the more than two thousand lesbian-themed mass-market books published in the 1940s, '50s, and '60s. Most of these books were written by men who had never knowingly seen a lesbian, much less spoken to one or given any serious thought to their lives. Nonfiction paperbacks like W. D. Sprague's surprisingly unbiased *The Lesbian in Our Society,* Lee Mortimer's scurrilous *Women Confidential,* or Jess Stearns's well-intentioned *The Grapevine,* all of which relied to some extent on real sociological fieldwork, were the exceptions to the rule. In general, lesbian-themed paperbacks were geared toward the prurient interests of a male readership that was content to imagine lesbians as castrating Amazonian warriors, frightened and confused women who just needed the love of the right man, pathetic male wannabes, or any number of other shallow and inaccurate stereotypes. Only one actual lesbian, Kay Addams, writing as Orrie Hitt, is known to

---

Ann Bannon. *Odd Girl Out.* Greenwich, CT: Fawcett Publications, 1957.
Ann Bannon remains the best known and most critically acclaimed author of lesbian paperback originals, primarily for her six-volume series devoted to Beebo Brinker and friends.

Ann Bannon. *I Am a Woman.* Greenwich, CT: Fawcett Publications, 1959.

Lee Mortimer. *Women Confidential.* New York: Paperback Library, 1961.
Hard-hitting, scandal-mongering tabloid newspaper columnist Lee Mortimer made a name for himself by suggesting that Frank Sinatra had connections with the Mafia. With his partner Jack Lait, Mortimer published a series of *Confidential* exposés of hypocritical American culture, including this shocker about "B-Girls," "He-Girls," and other wild women.

Kay Addams. *Queer Patterns.* New York: Universal Publishing and Distribution, 1959.
Addams also wrote under the name Orrie Hitt, and churned out roughly a book a month for several years in the late 1950s and early 1960s.

March Hastings. *Three Women.*
New York: Beacon Books, 1958.

March Hastings. *The Unashamed.*
New York: Midwood, 1968.

Donna Richards. *The Constant
Urge.* New York: Lancer
Books, 1966.

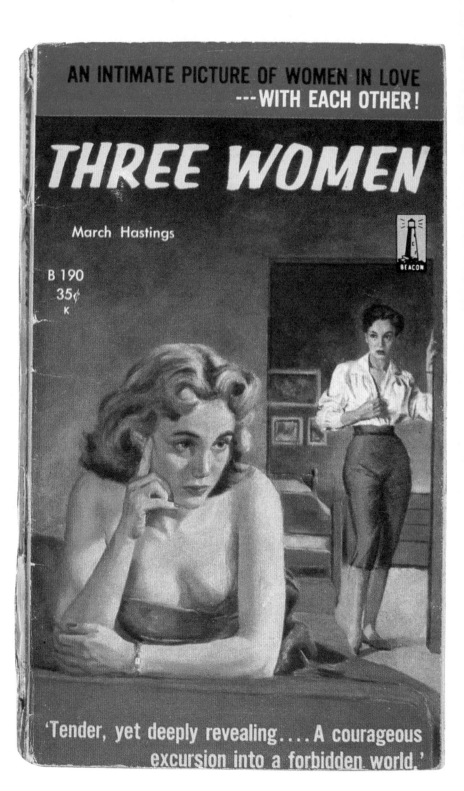

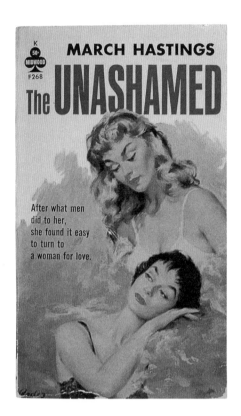 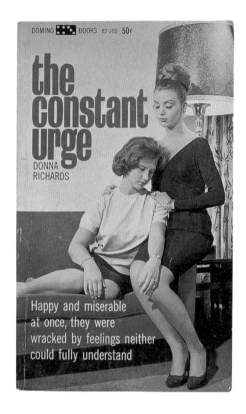

Lesbian Authors: Over a dozen actual lesbians wrote nearly a hundred novels between 1950 and 1965 that reflected contemporary lesbian lives with a degree of sympathy and realism.

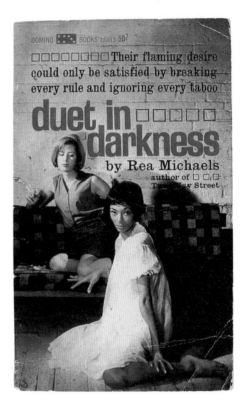

**Note the cover art on the books by Rea Michaels—
they are among the only representations of lesbians
of color in the entire lesbian paperback genre.**

Rea Michaels. *Cloak of Evil.* New York: Lancer Books, 1965.

Rea Michaels. *Duet in Darkness.* New York: Lancer Books, 1965.

Paula Christian. *The Other Side of Desire.* New York: Paperback Library, 1965.

have regularly churned out semipornographic sleaze novels for a predominantly male audience.

Harry Whittington, a widely published adventure writer capable of crafting well-paced page-turners, produced some of the better lesbian-themed fiction oriented toward a male readership. Lesbians in his stories tended to add an exotic element to the action-drenched plots, but they were not always superficial cardboard characters. In *Rebel Woman,* American Jim Patterson washes ashore in Cuba in the immediate aftermath of the revolution, only to discover that his former fiancée is now a communist military commando. Just as disturbing for our patriotic hero, she's romantically involved with her lovely lieutenant, Dolores. After being taken captive by his long-lost love, Patterson desperately tries to use his masculine charms to win his freedom. Revolutionary women with guns were definitely a favorite Whittington theme; he also wrote *Guerrilla Girls,* a reasonably taut adventure story set in Algeria, that involved its female narrator in a lesbian subplot.

Less polished than Whittington but still competent was Wenzell Brown, whose fascination with female criminals often led him to touch on lesbian themes. His *Prison Girl* tells the story of Linda, a woman in protective custody who has committed no crime, but who still faces the same horrible circumstances as any other woman behind bars. After hearing sadistic guards ravishing helpless prisoners in their cells, and seeing one too many formerly lovely face ripped apart by a switchblade knife, Linda finally decides to accept the protection of a "lady lover" who promises to keep her safe in exchange for sexual favors.

Some men, professional writers in search of a quick paycheck or new authors trying to break into print, wrote lesbian paperbacks strictly for the money, sometimes using female pen names. Lawrence Block, the award-winning author of the Matt Scudder mystery novels, got his start writing lesbian fiction under the names Jill Emerson and Sheldon Lord. Even then his writing was slick and serviceable, and he quickly moved on to other work. Other male authors made a career of writing lesbian novels, though usually of the semipornographic type, which required more persistence than talent to produce. Fletcher Flora was notable for half a dozen lesbian potboilers that were routinely better than those of his male peers, even if they did tend toward the melodramatic. His titles include *Strange Sisters,* a gruesome story about a young woman who experiences a mental breakdown after her involvement in three sadistic lesbian relationships, and *Desperate Asylum,* about a self-hating lesbian and a woman-hating man who commit marriage, murder, and suicide in rapid succession. Arthur Adlon turned out an average of three lesbian books a year between 1960 and 1965. All of his works offered what Bradley and Grier called a "short course in voyeurism," meaning that they found his books to have no redeeming features whatsoever. Don Holliday was even more prolific than Adlon. Besides penning dozens of campy gay male and bisexual swinger novels, he found time to write twenty trashy lesbian tales between 1959 and 1964. His work, at least, offered a playful sense of humor to leaven the predictable and obligatory sexual episodes that the formula required him to string along threadbare plots. By the time the golden age wound to a close in the mid-1960s, however, having a sense of humor about lesbian paperbacks was the most charitable stance one could take.

Harry Whittington. *Rebel Woman.* **New York: Avon Books, 1960.** Harry Whittington wrote reliable action fiction, including a few with lesbian themes, such as *Rebel Woman* and *Guerrilla Girls.*

Wenzell Brown. *Prison Girl.* **New York: Pyramid Books, 1961.** Brown made a career of writing about female criminals. *Prison Girl* told the tale of an innocent woman in protective custody who turns for safety to a "lady lover."

Arthur Adlon. *The Odd Kind.* **New York: Softcover Library, 1964.** Production values for lesbian paperbacks were not the highest in the publishing industry. Note the recycled cover art on *The Odd Kind* and *Unnatural Wife.* Authors Adlon and Carr were both noted for their production-line writing style.

Jay Carr. *Unnatural Wife.* **New York: Midwood-Tower Publications, 1962.**

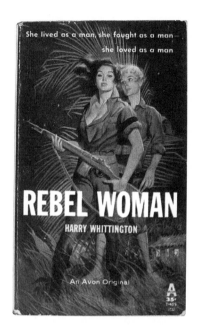

She lived as a man, she fought as a man—
she loved as a man

REBEL WOMAN
HARRY WHITTINGTON

An Avon Original

35¢

story of a woman behind bars

PRISON GIRL

Wenzell Brown

8795X K

THE ODD KIND

Arthur Adlon

UNVEILS THE SLEEK
AND EXPENSIVE
WORLD OF THE
LESBIANS WHO
MODEL FASHIONS IN
PUBLIC—AND
PERFORM AGE-OLD
RITUALS IN PRIVATE!

3rd BIG PRINTING

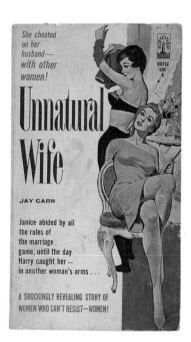

She cheated
on her
husband—
with other
women!

B933X
60¢
K

Unnatural Wife

JAY CARR

Janice abided by all
the rules of
the marriage
game, until the day
Harry caught her —
in another woman's arms . . .

A SHOCKINGLY REVEALING STORY OF
WOMEN WHO CAN'T RESIST—WOMEN!

Sheldon Lord [Lawrence Block].
69 Barrow Street. **New York: Tower Publications, 1959.**

Jill Emerson[Lawrence Block].
Enough of Sorrow. **New York: Tower Publications, 1965.**

Fletcher Flora. *Strange Sisters.*
New York: Pyramid Books, 1960.
Although *Strange Sisters* is probably referenced more often than any other work in the titles of books and articles on the lesbian paperbacks phenomenon, it's not a particularly memorable novel. The tale involves the mental breakdown of a young woman who has been in a series of abusive relationships with other women.

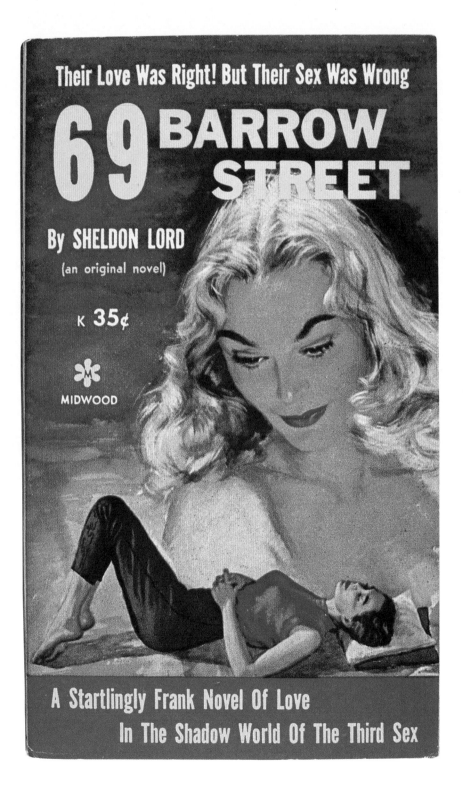

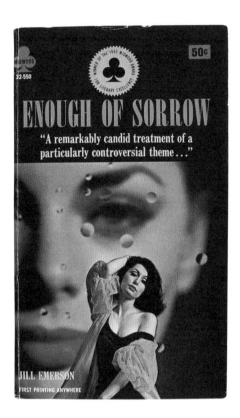

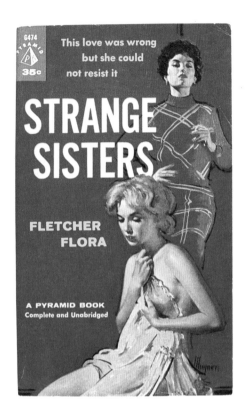

Award-winning mystery writer Lawrence Block, creator of the Matt Scudder series, got his start writing lesbian paperbacks under the names Sheldon Lord and Jill Emerson.

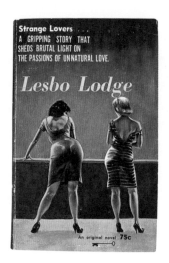

Most lesbian-themed paperbacks were written by men, for men.

They were exercises in titillation that had little to do with actual lesbian lives.

Here's a sample of some of the tackiest, in all their seamy splendor.

Harry Gregory. *Lesbian Web of Evil*. North Hollywood, CA: Brandon House, 1969.

Harry Barstead. *Lesbo Lodge*. North Hollywood, CA: Private Edition Books, 1963.

J. C. Priest. *Private School*. New York: Beacon Books, 1959.

Del Britt. *Flying Lesbian*. North Hollywood, CA: Brandon House, 1963.

Tony Trelos. *Cindy Baby*. North Hollywood, CA: Brandon House, 1964.

Love is a Many Gendered Thing

Christine Jorgensen. *A Personal Autobiography.* **New York: Bantam Books, 1968 (orig. pub. 1967).** Though she waited nearly fifteen years to publish her own autobiography, pioneering transsexual Christine Jorgensen's sudden celebrity in 1953 launched a wave of books and films about transgender subjects.

In December 1952, newspaper headlines shocked readers and provided fresh fodder for the paperback industry when they announced that twenty-six-year-old Bronx native Christine Jorgensen, formerly known as George, had just undergone sex-reassignment surgery in Denmark. The story of Jorgensen's transsexual operations was considered major news in papers around the world. As she herself commented years later in her autobiography, "It seems to me now a shocking commentary on the press of our time that I pushed the hydrogen-bomb tests on Eniwetok right off the front pages. A tragic war was still raging in Korea, George VI had died and Britain had a new queen, sophisticated guided missiles were going off in New Mexico, Jonas Salk was working on a vaccine for infantile paralysis—Christine Jorgensen was on page one." The journalism trade publication *Editor and Publisher* announced in the spring of 1954 that more newsprint had been generated about Jorgensen during the previous year than about any other individual—over a million and a half words, the rough equivalent of fifteen full-length books.

Jorgensen was not the first transsexual, but she certainly became the most famous one. News of her transformation coincided with a surge in public awe over scientific technology during the early days of the atomic age. The seemingly incredible tale of doctors changing a man into a woman offered yet another indication that science had indeed finally triumphed over nature—and raised questions in some quarters about whether science had finally gone too far. The massive media attention Jorgensen received, however, changed her life far more profoundly than had the surgeon's scalpel. Formerly a shy and largely unsuccessful commercial photographer who hid behind her camera, Jorgensen blossomed once the spotlight of sudden fame fell upon her. By the summer of 1953 she had fashioned her raw aptitude for holding an audience's attention into an engaging nightclub act, and she spent the next decade performing in venues throughout the world, often making as much as $5,000 a week. A wholesome beauty who had been built by science, a seemingly conventional woman who performed an unconventional sexual identity in the public sphere, a person whom many considered to be a gay man flaunting his sexuality behind a mask of feminine respectability—Jorgensen embodied many paradoxes of mid-twentieth-century American life.

The hectic pace of Jorgensen's stage career kept her far too busy to write a memoir until 1967. A paperback edition became a Bantam best-seller the next year, with more than a million copies in print. Others, however, were quicker to cash in on the Jorgensen phenomenon. Jorgensen had returned to the United States from Denmark in February of 1953 amid great fanfare drummed up by the Hearst papers, which began publishing a lengthy exclusive interview with her in five successive issues of their *American Weekly* Sunday supplement. In March 1953, Lion Books issued a paperback original that shamelessly exploited the Jorgensen hoopla, Cyril Kornbluth's *Half,* written under the pseudonym Jordan Park. *Half*'s back cover announced, "You've heard about 'men'" like the novel's protagonist Steven Bankow; "You've read about them in your daily newspapers. But here—*for the first time*—a novelist tackles the problem of a man who tries to change his sex." The cover blurb for *Half,* like much of the reporting on Jorgensen herself, conflated transsexuality (the desire to change sex) with hermaphroditism or intersexuality (being born with ambiguous genitalia). *Half* is actually the story of an intersexed baby raised as a boy, who begins to develop more pronounced female characteristics during adolescence and undergoes a surgical conversion operation to become a woman at age eighteen. Set in Chicago's South Side between 1925 and 1943, the book paints a portrait of working-class Polish-American life while chronicling a young person's struggle with sexual identity. Though apparently a work of fiction, the book is rich in historical and sociological detail and reads more like a thinly veiled biography than a novel.

The author of *Half* was familiar with the contemporary medical literature on sex changes. In one scene, Steven Bankow is in the Chicago Public Library, reading a medical treatise on "hypospadias with bilateral cryptorchidism," the congenital condition whose eventual diagnosis leads to his transformation into Stephanie. He stumbles across "an account of something called the Wegener-Sparre-Elbe case," which causes him to snicker incredulously and skip ahead in the text. Although the author does not elaborate further, the case referred to was a real one involving the former Einar Wegener, a Danish painter who adopted the name Lili Elbe and underwent a series of genital transformation operations, the last of which resulted in her death in 1931. The case received a great deal of media coverage in Europe, culminating in a biography by Niels Hoyer, in which Elbe is given the pseudonym Andreas Sparre, and which drew on Elbe's own diaries and medical reports. The book, translated into English and published by Dutton in 1933 under the title *Man Into Woman: An Authentic Record of a Change of Sex,*

Others, however, were quicker to cash in on the Jorgensen phenomenon.

WHAT WAS HIS BODY'S DARK SECRET THAT
MADE HIM NEITHER MAN NOR WOMAN?

A NEW NOVEL

25c

HALF

JORDAN PARK

This is the story of Steven Bankow. Born with life's most awful abnormality, openly taunted by his friends, secretly despised by his father, shamed by his own body—Steven Bankow walked the face of the earth, alone, ever seeking a path to happiness.

A LION ORIGINAL—
NOT A REPRINT

135

Jordan Park [Cyril Kornbluth].
Half. **New York: Lion Books, 1953.**
An effort to exploit the sudden attention called to transgender issues by Christine Jorgensen's celebrity, this novel features a hermaphrodite, raised male, who chooses to live as a woman and marry a man. It reads more like a thinly veiled biography than a work of fiction.

Niels Hoyer. *Man Into Woman.* **New York: Popular Library Edition, 1953.**
Originally published in English in hardcover in 1933, this book recounts the true-life tale of Lili Elbe—formerly the Danish painter Einar Wegener—who died shortly after undergoing sex-reassignment surgery in Germany in 1931. It was reissued in paperback twenty years later to cash in on the Jorgensen craze.

Stuart Engstrand. *The Sling and the Arrow.* **New York: Signet/ NAL, 1950.**
One of the first postwar novels to explore transgender themes, this potboiler about a tormented cross-dresser whose repressed homosexuality turns him into a wife murderer paved the way for later writers who worked the gender-bent psycho-killer plot line to far greater effect. The cover painting is by acclaimed paperback illustrator James Avati.

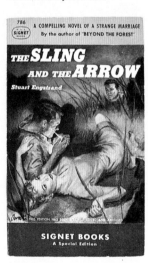

POPULAR LIBRARY 25¢ An Authentic Record Of A Change Of Sex

SP100

MAN INTO WOMAN

EDITED BY **NIELS HOYER**

This almost unbelievable book deals with the outstanding biological phenomenon of a man who changed his sex.

Complete and unabridged

was out of print for two decades until Christine Jorgensen's celebrity revived interest in the topic. The book was reissued in paperback by Popular Library in February 1953, a month before *Half*'s release.

Perhaps the best-known person to capitalize on Christine Jorgensen was transvestite moviemaker Edward D. Wood, Jr., famous in cult film circles as the "worst director in Hollywood," who was himself the subject of an Academy Award-winning Tim Burton film starring Johnny Depp. Only weeks after Jorgensen made headlines in 1952, Wood made his first significant foray into filmmaking. *Glen or Glenda?*, a deliriously serious defense of cross-dressing in which Wood himself starred as Glen, had been commissioned specifically as a cheap, unauthorized rehash of the Jorgensen story, but Wood turned it into an impassioned and deeply personal plea for tolerance of sexual diversity. The film contrasts the life of Glen, a heterosexual transvestite nervously contemplating a sex change, with that of a transsexual (Tommy Haynes, in the role of Alan/Ann) who decides to go all the way. In the end, the point seems to be that all Glen needs to find happiness is the love of a good woman who doesn't mind sharing her angora sweaters. Wood went on to make many other equally quirky films, including the stunningly inept *Plan 9 from Outer Space,* but he could never quite make ends meet as a director. Consequently, he wrote soft-core porn novels to supplement his meager income, including *Killer in Drag*

(1965) and *Death of a Transvestite* (1967). Wood died of a heart attack in 1978 at the age of fifty-four, two years before the rediscovery of his long-neglected work by a younger generation of movie fans.

Killers in drag and dead transvestites are staple themes in mass-market fiction about transgendered people. Two novels written in the late 1940s, well before the Jorgensen media blitz, suggest that transgender issues were actually quite central to postwar American anxieties about sexuality, and to the paperback phenomenon itself. Stuart Engstrand's *The Sling and the Arrow,* originally published in hardcover in 1947 and reissued in paperback by Signet in 1950, is notable for its early use of a now-familiar stereotype to address postwar shifts in gender relations—particularly the emotional costs of adhering to rigidly defined gender roles and expectations. Protagonist Herbert Dawes might well have been called "The Man in the Gray Flannel Skirt"—he is a sensitive, successful, happily married man who becomes a psychotic cross-dressing killer as a result of "the strains of contemporary competitive life" and "stresses left from his childhood." Engstrand's book drew on contemporary psychoanalytic ideas about the origins of homosexuality in repressed transgender identifications to gradually reveal the reasons why Dawes—a dress designer—keeps his short-haired wife Lonna outfitted

Ed Wood, Jr. *Killer in Drag.* **Union City, NJ: Imperial Books, 1965.** Skirt-wearing schlock-moviemeister Ed Wood, Jr., best known for his impassioned transvestite opus *Glen or Glenda?*, cranked out soft-core porn books to supplement his meager income as a filmmaker.

Ed Wood, Jr. *Death of a Transvestite.* **Aquora, CA: PAD Library, 1967.**

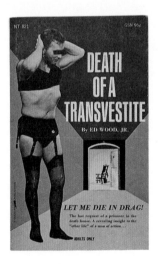

in slacks, doesn't mind when she has an affair with a burly sailor, and feels flashes of homicidal rage whenever she mentions wanting to have a baby. As a sympathetic psychiatrist explains to Lonna shortly before her untimely demise, self-hating Herbert Dawes unconsciously wants to be a woman to gain the love of his homophobic father and to revenge himself upon his meddlesome, domineering mother. He occupies himself professionally with women's clothes as an outlet for his suppressed transvestic desires. He fantasizes that Lonna is the man whom he wishes to love, but he also identifies with her as a woman and takes vicarious pleasure from her extramarital involvement with men. The prospect of becoming a father is a dose of reality that threatens to bring his dream world crashing down, and thus he harbors murderous thoughts about his wife as a last-ditch form of psychological defense.

Predictably, Dawes loses his tenuous grip on sanity. In a scene that could have been lifted straight from the pages of Kraft-Ebbing's nineteenth-century *Pyschopathia Sexualis* or Schreber's *Memoir of My Nervous Illness*, Dawes hallucinates that his body grows breasts and sheds "the loathsome cylinder of his masculinity." Soon thereafter he breaks Lonna's neck, raids his dress shop for some fetching postmortem attire, and drives off into the night where he takes his place near the head of a long line of gender-bent pop-culture killers, such as Norman Bates in Alfred Hitchcock's *Psycho* and Buffalo Bill in Daniel Harris's *Silence of the Lambs*.

The other representational convention of transgender identity—that of murder victim rather than murderer—provides the sensationalistic climax of *Vengeance Is Mine*, the third installment of Mickey Spillane's immensely popular Mike Hammer private eye series, published in hardcover by Dutton in 1950 and as a Signet paperback in 1951. Spillane's lyrically lurid stream-of-consciousness prose and his seamy plots helped sell more than fifteen million copies of his work by 1953 and came to epitomize the hard-boiled style. Spillane was a masterful storyteller, but his creation Mike Hammer was little more than a populist vigilante, a self-appointed guardian of middlebrow morality who expressed sadistic glee when gunning down commies,

queers, pimps, pill-pushers, and other criminalized outcasts rendered demonic by his reactionary imagination. "I love to shoot killers," he says in *Vengeance Is Mine*, "I couldn't think of anything I'd rather do than shoot a killer and watch his blood trace a slimy path across the floor."

More often than not, however, Spillane's killers turn out to be women—treacherous femmes fatale who spin murderous webs of deceitful intrigue until Hammer dispatches them with a cold, female-hating fury. In his first novel, *I, the Jury,* Spillane has Hammer pump a .45 slug into the gut of lovely Charlotte Manning—a dope-dealing psychiatrist at the center of a white slavery ring whom only pages earlier Hammer had intended to marry—as she stands naked before him in a futile attempt at seduction. When the dying Charlotte asks, "Mike, how could you do it?" Hammer chillingly replies, "It was easy." It's a theme played out repeatedly in Spillane's early novels: Hammer is transfixed by some fetishistic image of female beauty that he then violently destroys just when it threatens to become a desiring, flesh-and-blood person—a theme that sets up the transgender twist at the end of *Vengeance Is Mine.*

Hammer spends the second novel, *My Gun Is Quick,* pining after the fiancée he shot in *I, the Jury* and swearing to himself that he will never kill another woman. Then, in *Vengeance is Mine,* Hammer checks out a lead at an upscale modeling agency:

My mind couldn't get off the woman behind the desk. Some women are beautiful, some have bodies that make you forget beauty; here was a woman who had both. Her face had a supernatural loveliness as if some master artist had improved on nature itself. She had her hair cut short in the latest fashion, light tawny hair that glistened like a halo. Even her skin had a creamy texture, flowing down the smooth line of her neck into firm, wide shoulders. She had the breasts of youth—high, exciting, pushing against the high neckline of the white jersey blouse, revolting at the need for restraint. . . . Only then did I see the nameplate on the desk that read JUNO REEVES. Juno, queen of the lesser gods and goddesses. She was well named.

Mickey Spillane. *Vengeance Is Mine.* **New York: Signet Books/NAL, 1951.**
In his third Mike Hammer novel, best-selling Spillane makes use of a transgender character for a final plot twist.

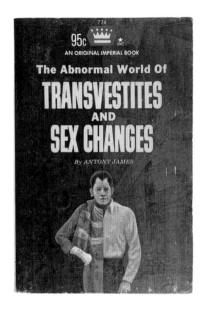

95c

AN ORIGINAL IMPERIAL BOOK

The Abnormal World Of

TRANSVESTITES
AND
SEX CHANGES

By ANTONY JAMES

(ADULT READING)

THE MALE LESBIAN

The bizarre case history of a man who actually lives the life of a Lesbian! *Myra Breckinridge* may be entertaining fiction, but this is the real thing!

BY "JILL" RANKIN
(AS TOLD TO ROGER BLAKE, PH.D.)

Sexless Lovers

LOVE METHODS OF EUNUCHS

Can there be sex without sex organs? The answer is yes. This book is a complete documentation of how eunuchs perform the act of sex. By John Midre-Pagnor.

LET ME DIE A WOMAN

THE WHY AND HOW OF SEX-CHANGE OPERATIONS

Hammer falls blindly in love with Juno, of course—so blindly, in fact, that he scarcely notices when she takes him to a "fag joint" in Greenwich Village, which should have been a dead giveaway that there was more to Juno than met the eye. When it becomes apparent that Juno's modeling agency is merely a front for a murderous blackmail operation, Hammer closes in, confronting Juno in her apartment. He knows she's the killer he's been searching for, but he is haunted by the image of Charlotte's bloody death and can't bring himself to pull the trigger a second time. Then Juno attacks him, and Hammer accidentally rips her dress off in the struggle. What he sees removes all his reservations about killing:

> I laughed through the blood on my lips and brought the Luger up. . . . The rod was jumping in my hand, spitting nasty little slugs that flattened the killer against the wall with periods that turned into commas as the blood welled out of the holes. . . . Juno died hearing all that, and I laughed again as I dragged myself over to the lifeless lump, past all the foam rubber gadgets that had come off with the gown, the inevitable falsies she kept covered so well. . . . I spit on the clay that was Juno, queen of the lesser gods and goddesses, and I knew why I'd always had a resentment that was actually a revulsion when I looked at her. Juno was a queen alright, a real, live queen. You know the kind. Juno was a man!

The differing treatments of transgender characters in The Sling and the Arrow and Vengeance Is Mine represent flip sides of the same coin. Though Dawes has been psychologically unmanned and Hammer is the very incarnation of hypermasculine machismo, both characters kill for the same reason—they each seek to ward off their own unten-able identification with a male homosexuality they despise. In the case of Dawes and other gender-disturbed murderers, their rejection of homosexuality is turned inward, against themselves, where it forces them to adopted a new gender position. In the case of Spillane and other homophobic killers, the rejection is directed outward, toward the transgendered figure itself. Simply by being desirable, the transgender person becomes a source of psychological terror that threatens the seemingly fragile heterosexual identity of the killer, and thus becomes the target of a murderous rage. That the representation of transgender figures capable of evoking such visceral reactions could be found in such popular paperback works offers a glimpse into the pressures many people must have felt to conform to social norms at the height of the McCarthy era. Of course, such representations had little to do with the lives led by real transgendered people.

Compared to gay, lesbian, and bisexual paperbacks, a disproportionate number of transgender titles told (or at least approximated) the stories of actual lives. Many were compilations of spurious "case studies," supposedly collected for their scientific value but actually intended for more prurient uses. The adult American reading public apparently found the facts of transgender identities and practices to be stranger (or perhaps more compelling) than any fiction. Antony James's The Abnormal World of Transvestites and Sex Changes (1965) seemed pretty tame in comparison to the more exotic erotica offered up in The Male Lesbian (1969), male-to-female transsexual Jill Rankin's journal of amorous escapades with other women, or in Sexless Lovers (1968),

Antony James. The Abnormal World of Transvestites and Sex Changes. New York: L. S. Publications, 1965.
One of the many paperback books that posed as a scientific treatise but actually offered salacious "case studies" for their readers' prurient interests.

Jill Rankin. The Male Lesbian. Cleveland, OH: Century Books, 1969.
Male-to-female transsexual lesbians do exist, but this book offers few insights into their lives. Instead, it provides another "case-study" that dwells largely on the details of the narrator's sexual fantasies and erotic practices.

John Midre-Pagnor. Sexless Lovers. Cleveland, OH: Classics Library, 1968.
"Can there be sex without sex organs?' The answer is a resounding yes! So says the author of this survey of the sex practices of eunuchs—males who have had their genitals removed through injury, illness, or their own wishes.

M. J. Lukas [Doris Wishman]. Let Me Die a Woman. New York: Rearguard Productions, 1978.
A promotional item distributed in conjunction with exploitation film-maker Doris Wishman's film Let Me Die a Woman, which included graphic footage of genital conversion surgery.

Not all transgender nonfiction aimed to arouse. Since

Christine Jorgensen's advent into popular consciousness, more than fifty transsexual autobiographies

have been published in book form, approximately one every year.

John Midre-Pagnor's treatise on "love methods of eunuchs." The author interviewed over two hundred individuals who had lost their penises to illness or injury. He found that some became transsexual, others the receptive partner in a gay relationship, but that most adopted erotic techniques for pleasuring women that have been popular with lesbians since time immemorial.

One of the more sensationalistic nonfiction titles was exploitation filmmaker Doris Wishman's *Let Me Die a Woman* (1978), which she wrote under the pseudonym M. J. Lukas as a promotional tie-in for her film of the same name, intending that the volume be sold by exhibitors in the theater lobby. *Let Me Die a Woman* had a stranger-than-fiction history that emerged from Wishman's pioneering nudist films of the early 1960s. Zelda Suplee, the woman who owned the nudist camp in Florida where Wishman shot most of her early films, later worked as a personal assistant to Reed Erickson, a fabulously wealthy female-to-male transsexual who had made his fortune extracting lead from old car batteries and selling it to the petroleum industry as a gasoline additive. Erickson privately funded a great deal of medical research on behalf of transgendered people, helping to establish the first university-based sex-change programs in the United States in the mid-1960s. Wishman and Suplee had remained friendly with one another, and the filmmaker was fascinated with her old collaborator's new line of work. Although packaged and promoted as a cheap exploitation title, the film version of *Let Me Die a Woman* actually contains rare historical footage of early transsexual support groups in New York, as well one of the first film documentations of an actual transsexual surgery. The book contains the life stories of many of the film's interviewees in addition to how-to information for prospective transsexuals.

Not all transgender nonfiction aimed to arouse. Since Christine Jorgensen's advent into popular consciousness, more than fifty transsexual autobiographies have been published in book form, approximately one every year. One of the first transsexual autobiographies to be issued as a paperback was *Roberta Cowell's Story* (1955). Cowell, a former Spitfire pilot in the Royal Air Force who had been shot down over Germany and finished out the war in a POW camp, told her remarkable tale with a typically British reserve. Unlike Jorgensen, she claims to have been an average male with unremarkable desires until, at age thirty-three, her body spontaneously began to change, rounding at the hips, blossoming in the bosom. Doctors told her the hormonally produced changes were irreversible. They suggested that since she would never again appear normatively male, she should complete the transformation through surgery and live the remainder of her life as a woman. Cowell took the news with a stiff upper lip, accepted her novel mission, and set about the task of becoming a woman with all the determination she had once shown in combat. She succeeded admirably, learning to shop and cook and dress and talk like her female compatriots. Cowell quietly completed her physical and legal transition to womanhood in 1951, eighteen months before news of Christine Jorgensen rocked the world. Only afterward did friends prevail upon her to tell her own story.

Coccinelle, the flamboyant star of a female-impersonation revue at the Carrousel Club in Paris, recounted the saga of her physical transformation to Italian journalist Mario Costa, whose *Reverse Sex* was published in Europe in 1962. Prolific soft-core porn writer Carlson Wade blatantly plagiarized Costa's work, reissuing the book in the United States under his own name but a different

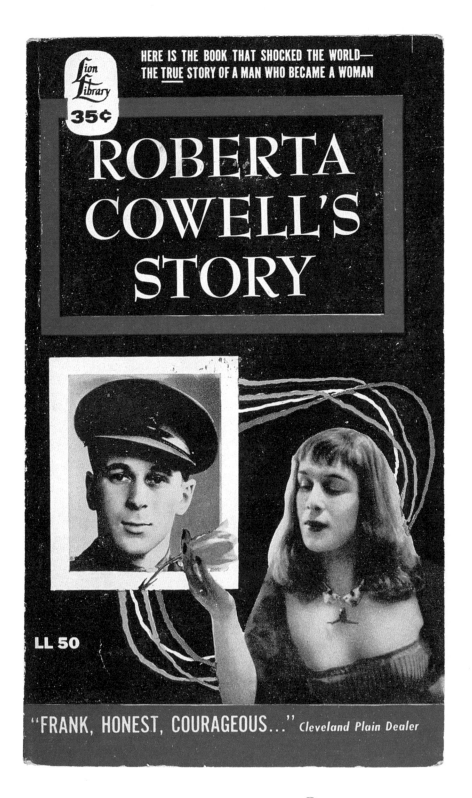

Roberta Cowell. *Roberta Cowell's Story.* **New York: Lion Books, 1955.** Cowell had been a British RAF pilot and POW during World War II, before claiming that she spontaneously began turning into a woman in the early 1950s. Surgery and hormone injections helped finish the job.

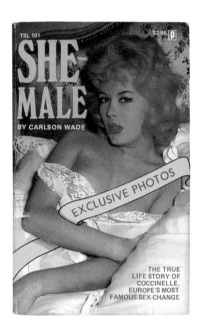

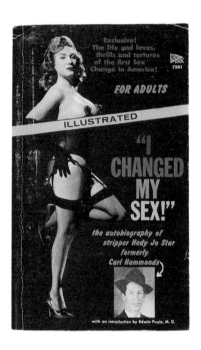

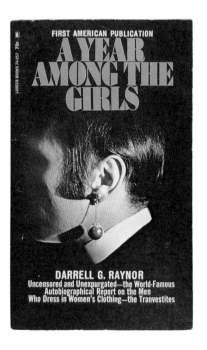

title, *She-Male*. Coccinelle, who had been born Jacques Charles Dufresnoy in 1935, looked remarkably like Bridget Bardot, the reigning French beauty queen. Her use of hormones and breast augmentation in the late 1950s reshaped not just her body but the field of professional female impersonation as well. Older performers complained that medical procedures like those employed by Coccinelle undermined the skilled craft-work necessary to create a compelling cross-gender illusion, but young performers rushed to emulate Coccinelle's hormone-enhanced verisimilitude. She continued to perform at the Carrousel Club even after her genital surgery and legal change of sex, blurring the boundaries between female impersonation and straight cabaret-style entertainment.

I Changed My Sex!, the audaciously titled autobiography of Hedy Jo Star, also saw print in the early 1960s. Star—who had been born Carl Rollin Hammonds in Prague, Oklahoma, in 1920—ran away to join the circus at age sixteen. After a brief stint playing the "Half Man-Half Woman" sideshow freak, she found her true calling as a strip dancer—no mean feat for a person whose body was at that point still unequivocally male. Star was a competent and determined businesswoman who owned her own multi-dancer strip show by the age of twenty-two. She not only danced herself but also choreographed the show, designed and sewed the costumes, built the sets, barkered the crowds, and booked the performances. After twenty years in show business, Star finally saved enough money for the medical procedures that had become widely known through the publicity about Christine Jorgensen. She began

taking hormones in 1956, but she was denied genital surgery by American doctors who considered the procedures unethical. In 1962, Star finally found a surgeon in Memphis, Tennessee, who would perform the operation. After retiring as a stripper, Star wrote an advice column for the *National Insider* tabloid in Chicago, and she finished her career as a costume designer for casino floor shows in Las Vegas.

Transsexuals were not the only people to write memoirs revealing the complexity of gender practices in mid-twentieth-century America. Kenneth Marlowe started his show-business career as a drag queen working in a Mafia-run Holiday Inn lounge in Calumet, Illinois. After a stint in the seminary where he trained for a mission to Africa, Marlowe eventually ran a lucrative out-call prostitution service that catered to Hollywood celebrities, and then worked as a hairdresser and hatmaker to the stars. He tells all in *A Madams Memoirs* [sic] (1965) and its equally dishy precursor, *Male Madam*. Darrell Raynor, in *A Year Among the Girls* (1966), supplies an insider's exposé of the furtive world of closeted heterosexual cross-dressers, who were only then beginning to form social organizations devoted to their secret pastime. Raynor's thoughts on the rapid emergence of a populous transvestite community in the early 1960s resonate with themes expressed in paperbacks twenty years earlier:

> *I think the stresses of our society, hanging as it has been since 1945 on the brink of some sort of atomic abyss, are creating more and more tensions among mankind. . . . Is it therefore any wonder that more and more men are finding relief by fleeing from their identity and the guilt of their war-crazy sex?*

Carlson Wade. *She-Male*. Wilmington, DE: Eros Publishing, n.d.
Prolific porn-writer Carlson Wade simply plagiarized Mario Costa's *Reverse Sex*—a biography of French female-impersonator-turned-transsexual Coccinelle—by putting his own name on the cover of the Italian journalist's work and changing the title.

Hedy Jo Star. *I Changed My Sex!* N.p.: Allied/Novel Book, n.d.
Born male in rural Oklahoma in 1920, Star ran away to join the circus, where she worked first in the freak show as a phony hermaphrodite, and later as stripper. After undergoing sex reassignment in the 1960s, Star became a newspaper advice columnist. She ended her career as a Las Vegas costume designer.

Kenneth Marlowe. *A Madams Memoirs* [sic]. Chicago: Novel Books, 1965.
This sequel to Marlowe's *Male Madam* offered further colorful reminiscences of the author's adventures as a professional female impersonator, prostitute, hairdresser, and milliner.

Darrell G. Raynor. *A Year Among the Girls*. New York: Lancer Books, 1968.
The author spent a year observing and participating in the heterosexual cross-dresser subculture of the early 1960s, where he met Virginia Prince and many other founding figures of that community.

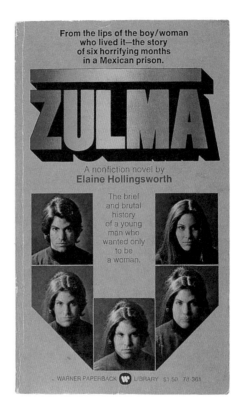

An unusually high proportion of transgender-related paperbacks were biographies and autobiographies. Publishers and the reading public apparently considered the facts of actual transgender lives to be stranger—or at least more compelling—than fiction.

Vivian Le Mans. *Take My Tool.* **Los Angeles: Classic Publications, 1968.**
This outrageously titled but visually unassuming paperback begins with a string of sexual escapades, but it also contains an extremely rare working-class transsexual autobiography spanning the 1930s through the 1960s in San Francisco, Los Angeles, and San Diego.

Elaine Hollingsworth. *Zulma.* **New York: Warner Books, 1974.**
This senselessly tragic story involves a charismatic young Mexican street queen in Tijuana who is befriended by the author shortly before being jailed for prostitution. Hollingsworth promised to pick up Zulma upon her release, but instead went shopping with her movie-star pal Yvette Mimieux. Zulma's body turned up a few days later in the city garbage dump.

Elsa Jane Guerin. *Mountain Charley.* **New York: Ballantine Books, 1968.**
The full title of this nineteenth-century true-life tale of the Wild West is *Mountain Charley: Or The Adventures of Mrs. E. J. Guerin Who Was Thirteen Years in Male Attire.* It is the only mass-market paperback published in the 1960s that explores female-to-male transgender themes.

Geoff Brown. *I Want What I Want.* **New York: Putnam Publishers, 1968.**
One of the better-quality literary treatments of transsexualism, British author Geoff Brown's novel was made into a film of the same name in 1972.

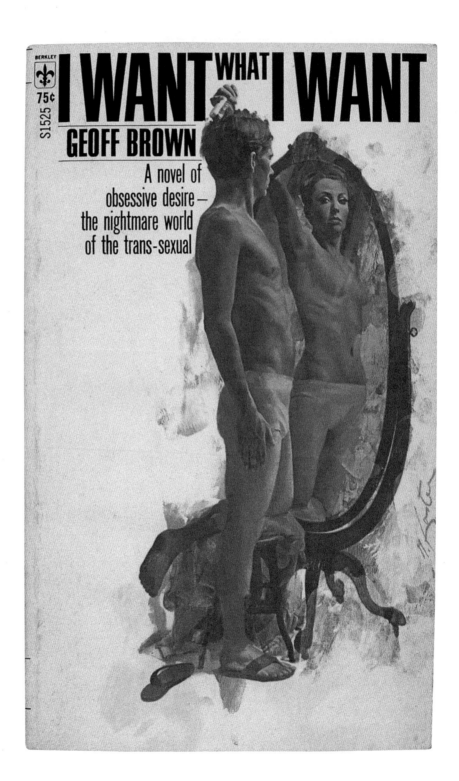

A few creditable literary treatments of transgender themes began to appear in paperback in the 1960s and '70s. Hubert Selby, Jr.'s *Last Exit to Brooklyn* (1960) and John Rechy's *City of Night* (1964) both offered haunting portraits of urban street queen subcultures. Later in the decade, Gore Vidal's *Myra Breckenridge* (1969), a farce in which the acclaimed author skewered contemporary relations between the sexes by following the exploits of his trans-sexual title character, became a mainstream best-seller. It was later filmed with Raquel Welch in the lead role. Transgender themes seem to have become radical chic during the same year when militant drag queens resisting police harassment sparked the Stonewall Riots in New York, paving the way for the gay liberation movement of the 1970s. Essex House, a small Southern California pub-lisher of erotica with avant-garde and countercultural tendencies, published a handful of transgender-themed books in the late 1960s: Jerry Anderson's *Trans* (1969), for example, and Hank Stine's *Season of the Witch* (1969), which featured a nonconsensual change of sex. Essex House also published the early work of Charles Bukowski and Phillip Jose Farmer and was known for its sophisticated sexual sensibilities.

A few other transgender titles from the '60s merit mentioning. Geoff Brown's *I Want What I Want* (1968), published earlier in England, offered a sympathetic portrayal of an upwardly mobile, working-class, male-to-female transsexual who toted around a copy of Simone de Beauvoir's *The Second Sex*. Like the famous French femi-nist said, "One is not born a woman, but rather, one becomes one." Ursula K. Le Guin's science-fiction classic, *The Left Hand of Darkness,* was first published in 1969. The story involves an alien race of beings who reproduce sexually, but who each change sex cyclically over the course of their individual lives. Le Guin was the daughter of eminent anthropologist Alfred Kroeber, a specialist in California's indigenous people, whose cultures often had more than two social genders. Le Guin grew up hearing family dinner–table talk about "berdaches," as gender-variant Native Americans were then called by anthro-pologists, and the perspective she gained from this knowl-edge of sexual diversity infused her work. Armistead Maupin's *Tales of the City,* begun in the 1970s as a news-paper serial in the *San Francisco Chronicle* and later published in book form, was a light diversion set in the city by the Golden Gate, whose cast of characters is presided over by warmhearted transsexual boarding-house operator Anna Madrigal.

Although books like *Tales of the City* reflected the increasing acceptability of transgender themes in literature and society, the bulk of transgender paperback fiction has nevertheless consisted of sheer sleaze, throwaway books designed for one-handed reading. The large number of such wickedly twisted, inventively plotted books suggests that kinky knots of fantasy and desire lurk just beyond the profit margins of mainstream commercial publishers. Sanford Aday's Fabian Books of Fresno, California, was one of the first sleaze publishers to tackle transgender content with its 1955 *Sex Gantlet to Murder,* by Mark Shane, which was reissued with a new cover in 1958 as *The Lady Was a Man.* Shane's novel involves a latently homosexual prison doctor who performs medical experiments that transform into a woman the handsome, heterosexual young criminal with whom he has become infatuated. The convict's body is altered but not his desires; "she" is still attracted to women, and she's rather upset that she's been forced into a sapphic lifestyle. Consequently, our heroine sets out to exact her revenge, becoming in the process an early literary example of the stereotypical lesbian serial killer. Arthur Adlon took a different tack in *All-Girl Office* (1965), casting his transsexual character as the object of lesbian desire. Lena Smith is an aggressive, lesbian business owner who prowls for sex among the ranks of her own employees and feels strangely attracted to new hire Gerry Powers. When Smith discovers that Powers is a preoperative transsexual, she somewhat improbably vows to restore Powers to manhood, become his wife, and live happily heterosexually ever after.

John Rechy. *City of Night.* **New York: Grove Press, 1964.**
This celebrated gay novel offers several gritty scenes drawn from the lives of street queens who frequented the Pershing Square neighborhood in Los Angeles.

Ursula K. Le Guin. *The Left Hand of Darkness.* **New York: Ace Books, 1976 (orig. pub. 1969).**
Le Guin's science-fiction classic about sex-shifting aliens was partly inspired by research on Native American gender systems conducted by her father, famed UC Berkeley anthropologist Alfred Kroeber.

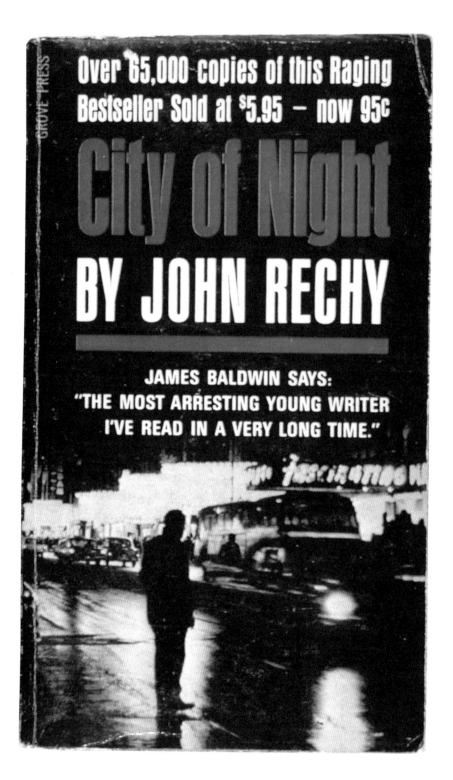

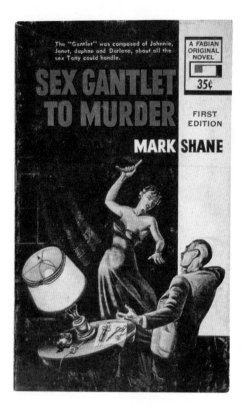

Transgender Sleaze

Mark Shane. *Sex Gantlet to Murder.* **Fresno, CA: Fabian Books, 1955.**
This early sleaze title offered readers a transsexual lesbian serial killer.

Arthur Adlon. *All-Girl Office.* **New York: Lancer Books, 1965.**
Arthur Adlon penned several lesbian paperbacks in the mid-1960s, but none more convoluted and improbable than this. Lena's a predatory dyke who runs her own consulting firm and seduces her female employees. She's strangely drawn to Gerry, who turns out to be a preoperative male-to-female transsexual. Lena decides to make a man of Gerry again so the two of them can get married and live happily ever after.

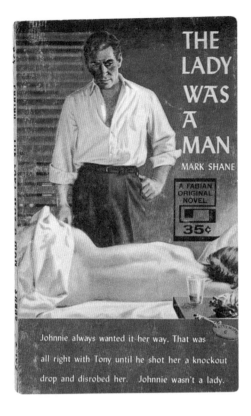

Mark Shane. *The Lady Was a Man.*
Fresno, CA: Fabian Books, 1958.
Sanford Aday's dogged Fabian Books
of Fresno, California, reissued its
steady-selling *Sex Gantlet to Murder* a
few years later under a new title.

Stark Cole. *The Man They Called
My Wife.* **North Hollywood, CA:
Brandon House, 1968.**
Brandon House was artier and more
avant-garde than most paperback
publishers.

Carl Corley. *Brazen Image.*
**San Diego, CA: Publisher's
Export Company, 1967.**
The story of a drag queen, intended
for a gay male readership.

Helene Morgan. *Queer Daddy.*
San Diego, CA: Satan Press, 1965.
The whole family goes to hell in this
over-the-top Oedipal nightmare from
Satan Press. Dad's a homo with the
hots for a tranny nanny, and Sonny
lusts after his sexually frustrated alcoholic mom while little sis gets it on
with the gardener. They don't make
them much queerer than this.

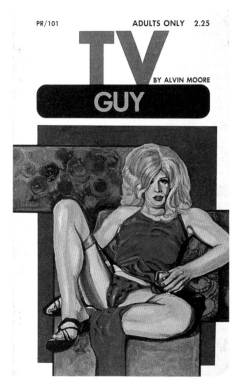

Sonia Tammy Taminoff. *Don't Call Me Eloise, Call Me Al.* **N.p.: Pixie Publications, 1973.**
It would be hard to imagine a cheaper cover illustration for this tale of a renegade housewife turned butch dyke biker.

Alvin Moore. *TV Guy.* **N.p.: Utopia Publications, 1975.**
A typical "one-handed reader" devoted to heterosexual male cross-dresser erotic fantasies.

It's a Gay, Gay, Gay, Gay World

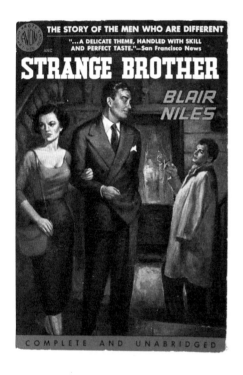

Blair Niles. *Strange Brother.*
New York: Avon Publishing, 1952
(orig. pub. 1931).
Blair Niles, a founding member of
the Society of Women Geographers,
was better known for her nonfiction
travel books. *Strange Brother* was her
only book involving gay themes, but
she treats Manhattan's homosexual
subculture much the same way she
does any other exotic locale.

Paperbacks exploring gay male themes have a different history than lesbian paperbacks, a history shaped much more directly by legal definitions of obscenity and by the differing values placed on male and female deviance from societal norms. Simply put, it has been far easier to construe the representation of gay male sexuality as inherently pornographic, which has had a tremendous effect on whether or not commercial publishers have been willing to publish work with explicitly gay content.

On the one hand, gay books in mid-twentieth-century America, when they were published at all, tended to be published in hardcover rather than paperback. This was due in part to the fact that men had an easier time than women accessing the more established routes to authorship, and also to the perceived need to bundle gay content with as many trappings of respectability as possible, in order to guard against charges of peddling mere pornography. As a consequence, some gay books had an easier time being accepted as daring but socially significant literature, rather than as exploitative middlebrow trash. On the other hand, a great deal of gay paperback writing has been pornographic, especially after 1965. Gay paperbacks of that era tended to be graphically sexual, focusing on erotic content at the expense of plot and characterization, and catering to an almost exclusively gay male audience. This stemmed in part from the demands of the readership accustomed to segregating their sexual expression from other aspects of their lives, whether by preference or due to homophobic oppression.

What is largely missing from the gay paperback genre is precisely what created and sustained the lesbian genre—a vast middle ground of mass-market books that portrayed issues of sexual diversity in a manner that could attract sexual minority audiences without alienating members of the cultural majority. Lesbian paperbacks flourished in part because they also appealed to men. Women in fiction, even lesbians, remain fantasy objects for heterosexual men's voyeuristic pleasures. The same is not true for gay men in literature, and the same mass market for gay-themed paperbacks never materialized. There was a flurry of gay paperbacks in the mid-1940s, but after that only a slow trickle of books appeared over the next twenty years. Not until legal standards of obscenity changed in the mid-1960s—the very changes that reshaped the paperback phenomenon itself and brought an end to its golden age—did gay paperbacks truly begin to flourish.

In marked contrast to the roughly two dozen lesbian novels published before 1945 that were reissued as paperbacks in the decade following World War II, only three pre-World War II novels with gay male themes were reprinted in paperback editions in the years between 1945 and 1955. It wasn't that novels with gay themes had not been published, but rather that those that did exist tended not to be reissued for the paperback market. While many of the lesbian novels were reprints of nineteenth-century French literature, all of the gay-themed paperback books had been written originally in the early 1930s, and all of them were set in New York City. These were Blair Niles's *Strange Brother* and André Tellier's *Twilight Men,* both published in hardcover in 1931, and Richard Meeker's *Torment,* originally published as *Better Angel* in 1933.

Historian George Chauncey suggests in his massive historical study, *Gay New York,* that the early 1930s were especially significant in the evolution of popular attitudes towards male homosexuality, in large part because of some unintended consequences of Prohibition. The constitutional amendment that made it illegal to produce or consume alcohol in the United States throughout the 1920s did little to affect the nation's drinking habits. It did, however, spawn a vast trade in bootleg liquor, which tempted otherwise straight-laced, law-abiding citizens to frequent illegal nightclubs known as speakeasies, where they were exposed to walks of life they might not otherwise have encountered had they been allowed to drink in the privacy of their own homes. Homosexuality, itself then a crime, was a visible part of the shadowy, criminalized nightlife created by Prohibition. In the jazz clubs and gin joints of Harlem and Greenwich Village, and in the nighttime entertainment districts of larger cities across the United States, a broad segment of the American population caught its first glimpse of gay urban subcultures.

Homosexuality, itself then a crime, was a visible part of the shadowy, criminalized nightlife created by Prohibition. In the jazz clubs and gin joints of Harlem and Greenwich Village, and in the nighttime entertainment districts of larger cities across the United States, a broad segment of the American population caught its first glimpse of gay urban subcultures.

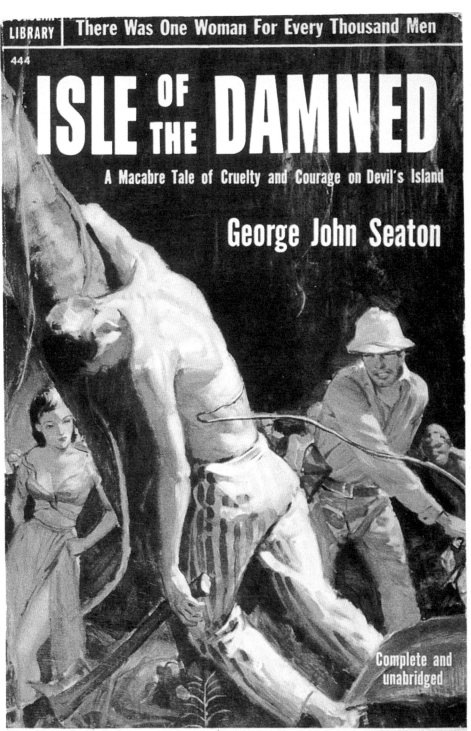

George John Seaton. *Isle of the Damned.* **New York: Popular Library, 1952.**
Devil's Island, the infamous French penal colony, gave more than one author an opportunity to explore the shocking extent to which men without women would engage in "situational homosexuality."

Blair Niles was one of those straight "sexual tourists" who went slumming in the gay demimonde of Manhattan. She was born Mary Blair Rice, the daughter of a prominent tidewater Virginia family whose roots stretched back to the colonial era. In 1902, she became the first wife of William Beebe, an adventurous, globe-trotting young naturalist and curator of birds at the Bronx Zoo, who years later made the first descent in a bathysphere into the ocean depths. Beebe and his bride frequently traveled abroad, and they co-authored two books about their experiences: *Two Bird Lovers in Mexico* (1905) and *Our Search for a Wilderness* (1908). The pair also visited the notorious penal colony on Devil's Island, which would figure in Blair Niles's later work. Between 1909 and 1911, the Beebes participated in a seventeen-month, 52,000-mile, twenty-two-country expedition across Asia to prepare a monograph series on wild pheasants. The rigors of the trip strained their marriage to the breaking point, however, eventually prompting Mary to depart for the wilds of Nevada, where she filed for divorce. The day after the divorce was granted, she married architect Robert Niles and dropped her given name Mary in favor of her middle name, Blair. It was as Blair Niles that she went on to considerable literary success, publishing sixteen travelogues, novels, and nonfiction books.

Strange Brother is set in New York, but Niles treats the homosexual subculture that serves as the story's backdrop in much the same way she treated any other foreign and exotic milieu. It is Niles's only work to focus explicitly on homosexuality, though the theme is suggested in her ongoing fascination with the behavior of men in the womanless world of Devil's Island. There is also a hint that some of the material may be drawn from autobiographical sources. The protagonist is a lonely young divorcée named June Westbrook, a writer whose ex-husband is gay. Westbrook befriends the emotionally tormented Mark Thornton, who is wracked by guilt over his attraction to other men. She accompanies him to any number of gay nightspots, including one in which Niles describes a performance by Gladys Bentley, the legendary tuxedo-wearing "Bull Dagger Who Sang the Blues," who was notorious for the way she openly flirted with and seduced the women in her audiences. Thornton eventually commits suicide, but through his death June learns to see "with a depth of focus which penetrates to the hidden places of the heart" that life can hold many forms of love.

While *Strange Brother* is really a novel about a heterosexual woman's platonic relationship with a gay man, André Tellier's *Twilight Men,* also first published in 1931, has a more pronounced gay male focus. Gay literary historian Roger Austin somewhat dismissively labels Tellier an "ersatz Proust" who simply transplants the great author's emphasis on the decadent, sordid, and desperate from fin-de-siècle France to depression-era Manhattan. The story involves Armand, an effete French poet with an aristocratic lineage, whose lover dies tragically at a young age. Armand sets sail for London, and later America, where he hopes to forget the past and drown his sorrows in an endless whirl of morphine, gay sex parties, and general dissipation. Armand's father, the Comte de Rasbon, suddenly appears on the scene, determined to save his wayward son from a life of terminal frivolity, even if this means committing him to a mental institution. Armand flies into a rage and kills his father, only to die soon afterward of a drug overdose.

Torment, by the pseudonymous Richard Meeker, is a sensationalized paperback repackaging of Forman Brown's classic coming-out tale, *Better Angel*. It tells the story of sensitive, handsome, and talented Kurt Gray, a musically inclined young man from small-town Michigan who is drawn into a gay relationship with college friend Derry Grayling. Derry is rather unmoved by their affair and palms Kurt off on a mutual friend, David Perrier, who has long been smitten with him. The plot becomes rather melodramatic; Kurt feels guilty that he enjoys David physically while remaining enamored of Derry. He then takes a final, futile stab at heterosexuality with Derry's sister Chloe. Eventually, Kurt establishes himself as a successful avantgarde composer in New York City, where he settles down with the man of his dreams.

In some respects, the novel parallels the biography of author Forman Brown, who was born in Michigan in 1901 and wrote *Better Angel* while touring in Europe in the

**André Tellier. *Twilight Men.*
New York: Pyramid Books, 1957
(orig. pub. 1931).**
One of several novels about male
homosexuality originally published
in the 1930s —along with *Strange
Brother, Butterfly Man, Better Angel,* and
Serenade—Twilight Men focuses on the
scenes of sex, drugs, and depravity
into which a young French aristocrat
throws himself to blot out the pain of
his lover's tragic death.

Harrison Dowd. *The Night Air.* **New York: Avon Publishing , 1953 (orig. pub. 1950).**
A poignant story about a broken man's realization that he can never recapture the lost innocence of his youth.

Only a few paperback reprints in the 1950s dealt directly with male homosexuality. It was far more common for gay authors to publish work that did not have explicitly gay content but that was informed by a gay sensibility . . .

1920s. Like Kurt and David, Brown and his life partner Roddy Brandon were both artists, master puppeteers who assumed creative control of the respected Yale Puppeteers group in 1929. They eventually settled the troupe into a permanent home at the Turnabout Theater in Los Angeles, where Brown lived until his death in 1995 at age ninety-four.

It was several years after World War II before the initial postwar wave of mainstream authors who dealt with gay subject matter began breaking into the ranks of mass-market paperback writers. Truman Capote and Charles Jackson were among the very first hardback authors to do so, both in 1949—Capote no doubt because the freshness of his youthful voice seemed worlds away from the war that had reshaped sexual mores, Jackson because he addressed so directly the inner emotions many men must have felt about the newfound, war-wrought visibility of homosexuality. John Horne Burns's *The Gallery,* originally published in 1947 and reissued as a paperback in 1950, was another work of fiction that tackled head-on the war-related shifts in American attitudes toward homosexuality. One story in this ensemble of tales, all set in Naples in the Galleria Umberto Primon in 1944, centers on Momma's Galleria bar, where gay soldiers and sailors from the Allied military forces come to drink and dish and cruise. At the center of the scene is Momma herself, a benevolent matriarch who presides over her establishment with tolerant affection:

> *Her crowd had something that other groups hadn't.*
> *Momma's boys had an awareness of having been born*
> *alone and sequestered by some deep difference from other*
> *men. For this she loved them.*

The other stories in *The Gallery* all revolve around hetero-sexual characters and story lines, but the book remains a landmark for the manner in which it simply acknowl-edged homosexuality as an objectively observable part of the social world without feeling the need to condemn it or moralize.

Gore Vidal's 1948 *The City and the Pillar* appeared in paperback in 1950. It quickly established itself as one of the definitive war-influenced gay novels, along with James Barr's *Quatrefoil,* which was published in hardcover in 1950 but not in paperback until the mid-1960s. Vidal's novel focuses on the life and loves of young Jim Willard, a high school tennis champ from Virginia who never thinks of himself as a homosexual, but who repeatedly finds himself in the arms of other men. He drifts into the merchant marines, and then drifts toward Hollywood, but he still finds himself unable to become romantically involved with women. He joins the army, then spends several years after the war making the rounds of all his former lovers, trying to understand and overcome the sense of loneliness and isolation that he cannot escape. In the end, he is finally able to confront his own desires and come to terms with his place in the world as a gay man.

Only a few paperback reprints in the 1950s dealt directly with male homosexuality. It was far more common for gay authors to publish work that did not have explicitly gay content but that was informed by a gay sensi-bility, such as the work of Paul Bowles or W. Somerset Maugham. One exception was Harrison Dowd's *The Night Air,* first published in 1950 and reprinted as a paperback in 1953. Its hero, Andy, is an alcoholic actor whose career is on the wane. He becomes disillusioned with the gay life in

Manhattan and grows nostalgic for his grandmother's farm in Vermont. It is a poignant story about a man remembering all the feelings that led him to leave home, recalling his loss of innocence and disillusionment and compromises, and mourning his inability to ever go home again.

It wasn't until later in the decade, when a new crop of writers began to publish work drawn from the experiences of men who had come to maturity in the postwar period, that homosexuality once again emerged in mainstream literature. Gerald Tesch's *Never the Same Again* (1958) written in a raw, unlettered style, focused on the explosive topic of intergenerational gay sex in small-town America. Johnny Parish is a lonely, curious, thirteen-year-old boy-next-door type who befriends Roy Davis, a thirtyish former sailor who has drifted into town and taken a job pumping gas. The two develop a relationship that, in spite of its physical nature, is emotionally innocent until Mr. Bently, the twisted scout master who has always secretly desired Johnny, creates a public scandal that leaves the whole town psychologically devastated. James Purdy, who developed a strong mainstream following in the mid-1960s, published *Malcolm* in 1959. For him, homosexuality was not the stuff of small-town scandal, but rather a shadowy undertone in an increasingly surreal postwar urban environment.

James Baldwin's *Giovanni's Room* (originally published in 1956) and Lonnie Coleman's *Sam,* both published in paperback in1959, offer opposite possibilities for gay men. Baldwin had been hailed as the best black writer of his generation for his *Notes from a Native Son*, but he felt that the effects of racism in the United States would never allow him to be seen simply as a writer, and he feared as well that being tagged as gay would mean he couldn't be a writer at all. Consequently, Baldwin spent much of his career in Europe. *Giovanni's Room* deals with an American man in Europe who is torn between following his heart, which would mean making a life with an Italian bartender to whom he is deeply attracted, and caving in to social pressure to marry his American girlfriend. The book reflects on many levels Baldwin's own sense of alienation from the culture that produced him. The title character of Lonnie Coleman's *Sam,* on the other hand, has definitely found his niche. He is a thirty-something publisher who enjoys his work and has a great apartment in Manhattan. He's in the process of breaking up with one boyfriend, who refuses to let their relationship deepen, and courting another, who promises to be somebody with whom he could grow old. Sam is surrounded by a circle of friends, both gay and straight, whose problems create most of book's drama. Though the book seems a bit dated in places, it remains a readable reminder that some gay men had plenty of self-esteem and healthy relationships long before the gay liberation movement of the later 1960s.

Gay-themed paperback originals started appearing about the same time as their lesbian counterparts, but once again, as was the case with hardcover reprints, in far fewer numbers. *Men into Beasts,* published in 1952, was among the first. It was a nonfiction book that dealt in part with "situational homosexuality" in prison. Its author, George Viereck, a minor poet who ran in avant-garde circles

Gerald Tesch. *Never the Same Again.* **New York: Pyramid Books, 1958.** This crudely-written story tackles the explosive issue of intergenerational gay sex. It's not the boy and his transient soldier friend who seem morally reprehensible, however—it's the twisted scoutmaster who wants little Johnny for himself and creates a scandal that tears a town apart.

James Purdy. *Malcolm.* **New York: Avon Publishing, 1959.** Purdy gained a cult following in the later 1960s for his surreal tales of urban life, in which homosexuality was just part of the mix.

James Baldwin. *Giovanni's Room.* **New York: Signet Books, 1959.** James Baldwin was the most-read black American author of the twentieth century, but he chose emigration to Europe over being pigeonholed as a minority writer. *Giovanni's Room,* ostensibly a story about an American student torn between an Italian bartender and the woman he is supposed to marry, works on many levels to express Baldwin's alienation from his own society and his determination to write on universal themes.

Lonnie Coleman. *Sam.* **New York: Pyramid Books, 1959.** Coleman created a surprisingly well-rounded, well-adjusted, happy and successful title character in this story of a gay New York publisher and his circle of friends.

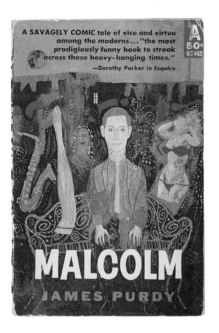

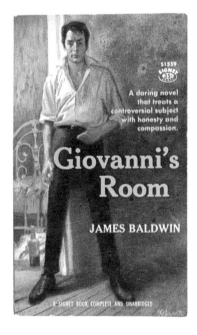

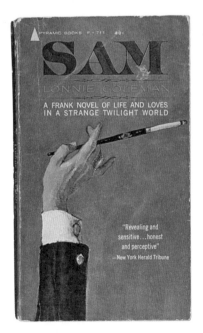

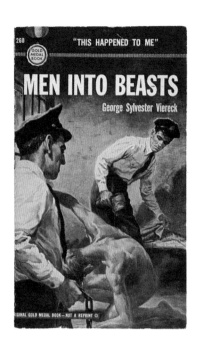

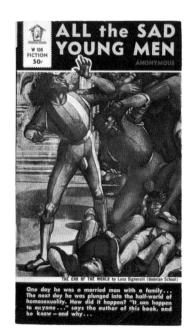

before World War I, had been born to German parents but was raised in New York City. He became something of a black sheep for his chauvinistic support of the Kaiser. His intense German nationalism landed him in hot water again during World War II, when he publicly expressed his admiration for Hitler and was sent to prison. Two other gay PBOs, David Karp's *Brotherhood of Velvet* and Dyson Tayler's *Bitter Love,* were also published in 1952, and both treated men involved in triangles with a woman and another man.

Prior to the mid-1960s, there simply were no mass-market books that dealt with male-male desire that did not somehow couch it in terms of bisexual conflict, illustrate it with misleading cover art containing both men and women, or hide it behind pathologizing marketing blurbs. This was certainly the case with *Whisper His Sin,* by Vin Packer (a.k.a. Marijane Meaker), published in 1954, which did a little of all three. To quote the back cover copy, the book "deals with a strange way of life that has become all too prevalent and is still spreading . . . a frightening picture of how the blight of sexual distortion spreads, corrupts, and finally destroys those around it."

A steady trickle of gay male paperback originals continued to appear throughout the 1950s and early 1960s. Ronn Marvin's *Mr. Ballerina* was published in 1961, followed by *All the Sad Young Men* in 1962. The latter was a cheeky, anonymously written, thinly fictionalized novel about Jean Hayes, a New York society columnist "whose husband is, to put it mildly, considerably more of a lady than she." In 1963, Kozy Books published *Male Bride,* the first paperback original aimed at a gay male audience that had a brazen, unmistakably gay image on the cover. By 1964, half a dozen such books had appeared from various publishers, including James Colton's *Lost on Twilight Road* and Ed Culver's *Kept Boy,* about an accomplished though occasionally overbearing Manhattan interior decorator who has a falling out with his beautiful boy-toy, Carl, during a weekend on Fire Island. Thinking he can do better elsewhere, Carl looks for love in all the wrong places before discovering that there really is no place like home.

After 1964, the pace of gay publishing picked up quickly. According to Tom Norman's bibliography of American gay erotic paperbacks, thirty gay paperback books were published in 1965, and over a hundred in 1966. Only a few of these mid-'60s titles were reprints of older novels, such as *Teleny, or the Reverse of the Medal,* a gay erotic work from the 1890s long attributed to Oscar Wilde. Also published at this time were *Quatrefoil* (1965), and *Butterfly Man* (1967). The latter novel, by Lew Levenson, had originally been published in 1934. Like most other gay novels written before World War II, it was an overwrought, hand-wringing melodrama. This one at least had a lively plot involving Ken Gracey, a Texas high school basketball star turned dancer, who is held virtually hostage by an older, amoral homosexual named Mr. Lowell who happens to hold the mortgage on the young man's family farm. The younger man is spirited away to the fleshpots of Malibu Beach, where he becomes tainted by exposure to a dissolute lifestyle. Gracey starts performing in drag shows, gets raped in Chicago by members of Al Capone's gang, becomes alcoholic, contracts a venereal disease, and winds up in a New York jail. There he meets nice girl who tries to save him, but it is too late—upon his release he wanders in an alcoholic stupor into the East River and drowns. On the other hand, James Barr's *Quatrefoil,* first

George Sylvester Viereck. *Men Into Beasts.* **Greenwich, CT: Fawcett Publications, 1952.**
This memoir by George Viereck, a bohemian poet whose support for Germany in both world wars landed him in prison, has the distinction of being the first American paperback original to deal with male homosexuality.

Vin Packer [Marijane Meaker]. *Whisper His Sin.* **Greenwich, CT: Fawcett Publications, 1954.**
As Vin Packer, lesbian author Marijane Meaker usually wrote stories about crime and juvenile delinquency. This potboiler about a man's homosexual leanings was an exception.

Anonymous. *All the Sad Young Men.* **New York: Wisdom House, 1962.**
This anonymously written paperback original strayed dangerously close to libel in its thinly disguised descriptions of a society columnist whose husband had a penchant for other men.

Ronn Marvin. *Mr. Ballerina.* **Evanston, IL: Regency Books, 1961.**
One of several paperback originals dealing with homosexuality to appear in the early 1960s.

Oscar Wilde. *Teleny, or The Reverse of the Medal.* Chatsworth, CA: Brandon Books, 1966 (orig. pub. 1893). Wilde supposedly wrote this gay erotic story several years before his infamous trial for sodomy; it enjoyed a long career as an underground classic before being reprinted in paperback in the mid-1960s.

James Barr. *Quatrefoil.* New York: Paperback Library, 1965 (orig. pub. 1950). Though it took fifteen years to appear in paperback, *Quatrefoil* was regarded as one of the best mid-twentieth-century novels to explore the effects of World War II on the lives of gay men.

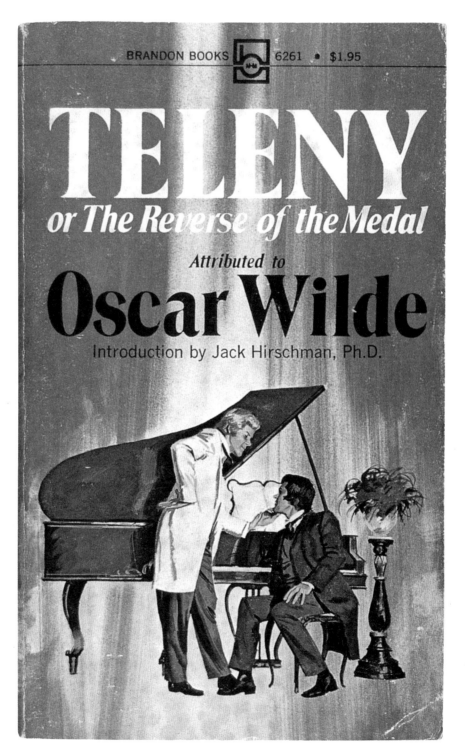

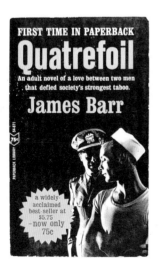

published in 1950, was a relentlessly positive book, its characters as upbeat as Levenson's were downtrodden. Phillip and Tim are naval officers who meet in Seattle in 1946 and fall in love. They are wealthy, well-educated, multi-lingual, sophisticated men who consider themselves morally superior to most homosexuals, whom they see as always tending to slide into degeneracy. Tim is killed in a plane crash, but Phillip overcomes his grief and determines to make the best of life.

Most of the new gay books appearing in the mid-1960s were paperback originals, rather than reprints, and most were explicitly pornographic. Landmark court cases from the late 1950s through the mid-1960s involving *Lady Chatterly's Lover, Portnoy's Complaint,* and *Naked Lunch* had set new legal standards for obscenity. The new rulings shifted obscenity from the subjective realm of "I know it when I see it," which more or less allowed law enforcement officers to file charges against anything they personally objected to, to more liberal criteria involving "community standards" and whether or not sexually explicit material had any "redeeming social value." Representations of gay sexuality were initially considered to have no redeeming social value, but as these new standards were interpreted in case law over the second half of the 1960s, they were found to provide a very broad range of protection for many kinds of published material that had previously been considered unprintable, including gay erotica. Whereas the majority of pre-1965 gay paperbacks had at least attempted to be socially realistic, most of what was published after that was sheer sexual wish-fulfillment fantasy.

Gay porn publishing had its roots in the body-builder photo magazines—the so-called "physique pictorials"—of the early 1950s. The most notable of these were the Grecian Guild publications of H. Lynn Womack, a former Georgetown University philosophy professor who championed First Amendment freedoms while building a gay porn empire. Womack won an important legal victory in 1961, when he successfully sued the postmaster general of the United States for seizing copies of his physique magazines. In 1962 Womack founded Guild Press, a mail-order book service that offered gay men many of the gay-themed paperbacks that had appeared since World War II, and which eventually began publishing its own original titles. Most Guild Press publications were incredibly cheaply produced, usually in pamphlet or booklet form rather than as actual bound books, and all were concerned primarily with representing gay male sexual experiences for a gay male readership. Most titles weren't particularly memorable,

Phil Andros [Sam Steward]. *When in Rome Do...* **[San Francisco]: Gay Parisian Press, 1971.**
Sam Steward was a genius among hacks, who wrote brilliantly of his life as gay hustler Phil Andros.

James J. Proferes. *Hellbound in Leather.* **Washington, DC: Guild Press, 1966.**
Proferes wrote many of the original titles published by the trailblazing Guild Press, which had published gay-oriented physique magazines in the 1950s. In 1962 Guild won an important legal victory to distribute publications with gay erotic content.

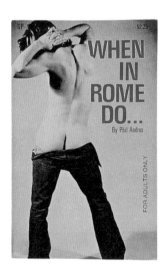

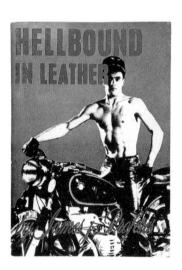

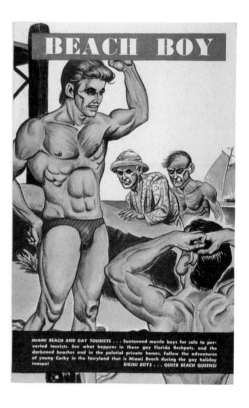

When more liberal interpretations of obscenity laws began to be upheld in the mid-1960s, gay porn publishing exploded. Unlike most books written prior to 1965, which tended to depict homosexuality with a degree of social realism, most gay paperbacks published after 1965 were sheer sexual wish-fulfillment fantasies.

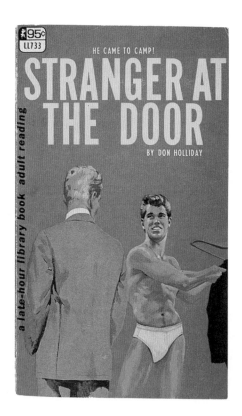

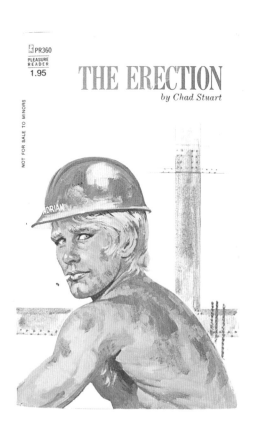

Peter Sinnott. *Young Danny*. N.p.:
Unique Books, 1966.

Donald Evans. *Beach Boy*. New
York: Selbee Publications, 1966.

Don Holliday. *Stranger at the
Door*. San Diego, CA: Phenix
Publishers, 1967.

Chad Stuart. *The Erection*.
San Diego, CA: Greenleaf
Classics, 1972.

Lynton Wright Brent. *Sir Gay*.
Hollywood, CA: Brentwood
Publishing, 1965.

Gene North. *Skid Row Sweetie*.
San Diego, CA: Phenix
Publishers, 1968.

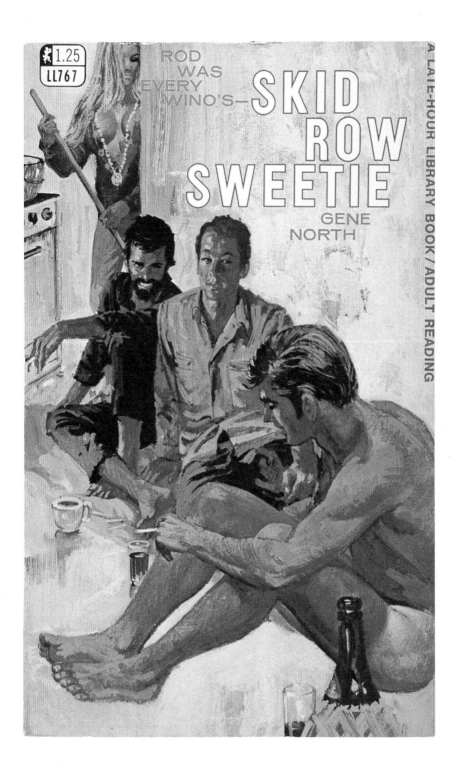

Don Holliday. *The Man From C.A.M.P.* San Diego, CA: Corinth Publications, 1966.

Ray Douglas, Jr. *Passion to Disaster.* Fresno, CA: National Library Books, 1969.

Michael Scott. *The Killer Queens.* San Diego, CA: Corinth Publications, 1968.

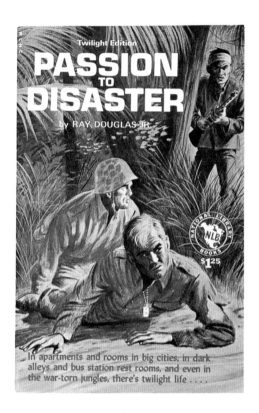

Many gay paperback porn titles from the later 1960s played into the conventions of male genre fiction— sometimes spoofing them viciously. There were gay detective stories, gay war stories, gay spy thrillers, and stories featuring gay mercenaries and fortune hunters.

Richard Amory [Richard Love].
Song of the Loon. San Diego, CA:
Greenleaf Classics, 1968.
Richard Amory's Loon trilogy is reput-
edly the most widely read work of gay
American fiction—so popular that it
spawned its own parody, Fruit of the
Loon. The books painted a pastoral
picture of loving harmony between
white men and native Americans in a
mythical Wild West.

Ricardo Armory. *Fruit of the
Loon.* San Diego, CA: Greenleaf
Classics, 1968.

but a few gems stood out, like *$tud,* by Sam Steward, writing under the name Phil Andros about his life as a male hustler. Steward, who held a Ph.D. in English and had befriended Gertrude Stein and Alice B. Toklas in Paris, was something of an underground legend. He really did work as a hustler and tattoo artist, and his descriptions of the seamier sides of urban gay culture compare favorably with those of Jean Genet.

By the later 1960s, gay porn novels catered to most every taste in men's genre fiction: there were gay Westerns, gay detective stories, gay spy thrillers, gay war stories, gay prison fiction. Many of these books offered campy spoofs of generic conventions, though some were distinguishable from their straight counterparts only to the extent that they substituted explicit homosexual sex acts for the muted homosocial bonding so prevalent in men's fiction. One particularly prolific author for Greenleaf Classics, which published some of the better gay porn of the later 1960s, was Chris Davidson, who made a career of exploring various sexual taboos in his work. His *Different Drums* (1967) dealt with a gay relationship between a Northern and a Southern soldier during the Civil War. *Go Down, Aaron* (1967) was about a Jewish sex slave in Nazi Germany, while *Caves of Iron* (1967) told the story of a prison romance between a gay doctor convicted on a sodomy charge and a young first-time convict.

Another successful author for Greenleaf was Richard Amory, whose *Song of the Loon,* published in 1966, has been described as a gay version of *The Last of the Mohicans,* as well as a "gawky yoking of Andre Gide and Louis L'Amour." Amory himself classified his novel and its two sequels, *Song of Aaron* (1967) and *Listen, the Loon Sings* (1968), as pastoral fiction, in which he portrays an idealistic union between Native Americans and Euro-Americans, set in a mythic West where everything is fraught with sexual meaning and erotic possibilities. In spite of its shortcomings as literature, the Loon trilogy was profoundly influential, particularly in its affirmation of gay sexuality for a wide gay readership. In this respect it can be considered an early example of the gay liberation ideology that erupted a few years later at the Stonewall Inn in Greenwich Village. One scholar of gay fiction estimates that approximately one-third of all adult gay men in the United States have read the first Loon novel.

Greenleaf was only one of a number of gay porn publishers that emerged in the 1960s, each with its own individual style. Greenleaf tended to be more literary and even dabbled in avant-garde trendiness, publishing books

Chris Davidson. *Caves of Iron.* **San Diego, CA: Greenleaf Classics, 1967.**
Chris Davidson wrote regularly for Greenleaf Classics, one of the more literary of the gay porn publishers. Many of his books were historical fiction that, if nothing else, attempted to show that gay men had existed in times other than the present. They also tended toward sadomasochistic themes. *Go Down, Aaron* was set in Nazi Germany, while *Caves of Iron* was set in a contemporary California prison.

Chris Davidson. *Go Down, Aaron.* **San Diego, CA: Greenleaf Classics, 1967.**

like Jeff Lawton's *Truck Stop* (1969), which read like a William Burroughs cut-up novel and was printed in a skewed, rotated, and oddly spaced type. Brandon House, which published a wide range of sexually explicit material including gay erotica, had countercultural sympathies and seems to have viewed gay books as just another facet of the sexual revolution. Publisher's Export Company in San Diego, California, showed a lot of spunk with some of its early offerings in the mid-1960s, which tended to have interesting cover art and clever titles such as Bert Shrader's *Fee Males* and Mark Dunn's *Queer Guise*. By the 1970s, however, their books had become entirely formulaic. Altogether, there were at least twenty publishers of gay porn in the late 1960s, ranging in quality from Neva Paperbacks in Las Vegas, which never rose above the most conventional and predictable exploitation fare, to Olympia Press, the prestigious Parisian publisher of Henry Miller, Anaïs Nin, Vladimir Nabokov, and Samuel Beckett, which relocated to New York in 1967 to take advantage of the more liberal publishing environment in the United States.

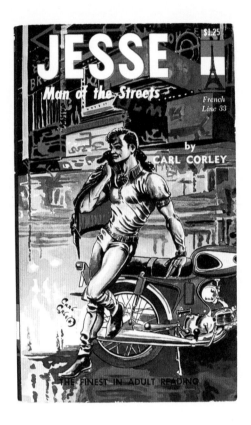

Publisher's Export Company (PEC) produced some of the most interesting covers of all the late-1960s gay porn. *Jesse* was one of the very best. In spite of the psychedelic overtones, *Gay Stud's Trip* was about hitchhiking, not LSD. Carl Corley and Bert Shrader were regular authors for PEC's French Line series.

Carl Corley. *Jesse, Man of the Streets*. San Diego, CA: Publisher's Export Company, 1968.

Bert Shrader. *Gay Stud's Trip*. San Diego, CA: Publisher's Export Company, 1968.

Bibliography

Citations for Works Illustrated

Addams, Kay. *Queer Patterns*. New York: Universal Publishing and Distribution, 1959.

Adlon, Arthur. *All-Girl Office*. New York: Lancer Books, 1965.

———. *The Odd Kind*. New York: Softcover Library, 1964.

Aldrich, Ann [Marijane Meaker]. *We Walk Alone*. Greenwich, CT: Fawcett Publications, 1955.

Amory, Richard [Richard Love]. *Song of the Loon*. San Diego, CA: Greenleaf Classics, 1968.

Andros, Phil. [Sam Steward]. *When in Rome Do . . .* [San Francisco]: Gay Parisian Press, 1971.

Anonymous [Daoma Winston]. *Adam and Two Eves*. New York: Royal Books, ca.1953 (orig. pub. 1924).

Archer, Marion. *Thrill Chicks*. New York: Bee-Line Books, 1969.

Armory, Ricardo. *Fruit of the Loon*. San Diego, CA: Greenleaf Classics, 1968.

Baldwin, James. *Giovanni's Room*. New York: Signet Books, 1959.

Bannon, Ann [Ann Thayer]. *I Am a Woman*. Greenwich, CT: Fawcett Publications, 1959.

———. *Odd Girl Out*. Greenwich, CT: Fawcett Publications, 1957.

Barr, James. *Quatrefoil*. New York: Paperback Library, 1965 (orig. pub. 1950).

Barstead, Harry. *Lesbo Lodge*. North Hollywood, CA: Private Edition Books, 1963.

Blake, Bob. *Gay Gay a Go-Go*. Aqoura, CA: PAD Library, 1966.

Bowles, Paul. *The Sheltering Sky*. New York: Signet Books/NAL, 1951.

Box, Edgar [Gore Vidal]. *Death in the Fifth Position*. New York: Signet Books, 1953.

Bradley, Marion Zimmer, and the Friends of Darkover. *Free Amazons of Darkover*. New York: Daw Books, 1985.

Brent, Lynton Wright. *Lavender Love Rumble*. Hollywood, CA: Brentwood Publications, 1965.

———. *Sir Gay*. Hollywood, CA: Brentwood Publications, 1965.

Britain, Sloane. *First Person, 3rd Sex*. Chicago: Newsstand Library, 1959.

Britt, Del. *Flying Lesbian*. North Hollywood, CA: Brandon House, 1963.

Brock, Lilyan. *Queer Patterns*. New York: Eton [Avon], 1952.

Brown, Geoff. *I Want What I Want*. New York: Putnam Publishers, 1968.

Brown, Wenzell. *Prison Girl*. New York: Pyramid Books, 1961.

Cain, James. M. *Serenade*. New York: Signet Books/NAL, 1954 (orig. pub. 1937).

Capote, Truman. *Other Voices, Other Rooms*. New York: Signet Books/NAL, 1949.

Christian, Paula. *The Other Side of Desire*. New York: Paperback Library, 1965.

Clifton, Bud. *Muscle Boy*. New York: Ace Books, 1958.

Cole, Stark. *The Man They Called My Wife*. North Hollywood, CA: Brandon House, 1968.

Coleman, Lonnie. *Sam*. New York: Pyramid Books, 1959.

Colton, James. *Lost on Twilight Road*. Fresno, CA: National Library Books, 1964.

Corley, Carl. *Brazen Image*. San Diego, CA: Publisher's Export Company, 1967.

———. *Jesse, Man of the Streets*. San Diego, CA: Publisher's Export Company, 1968.

Cowell, Roberta. *Roberta Cowell's Story*. New York: Lion Books, 1955.

Crane, Clarkson. *Frisco Gal*. New York: Diversey Publishing, 1949.

Davidson, Chris. *Caves of Iron*. San Diego, CA: Greenleaf Classics, 1967.

———. *Go Down, Aaron*. San Diego, CA: Greenleaf Classics, 1967.

Delany, Samuel R. *The Ballad of Beta-2.* New York: Ace Books, 1965.

Devlin, Barry. *Forbidden Pleasures.* New York: Berkley Publishing, 1953.

Douglas, Dean. *Man Divided.* New York: Fawcett Publications, 1954.

Douglas, Ray, Jr. *Passion to Disaster.* Fresno: National Library Books, 1969.

Dowd, Harrison. *The Night Air.* New York: Avon Publishing, 1950.

Emerson, Jill [Lawrence Block]. *Enough of Sorrow.* New York: Tower Publications, 1965.

Engstrand, Stuart. *The Sling and the Arrow.* New York: Signet/NAL, 1950.

Evans, Donald. *Beach Boy.* New York: Selbee Publications, 1966.

Fenster, Percy. *Hot Pants Homo.* North Hollywood, CA: All Star Books, 1964.

Flora, Fletcher. *Strange Sisters.* New York: Pyramid Books, 1960.

Geddes, Donald Porter, and Enid Curie. *About the Kinsey Report.* New York: Signet Books, 1948.

Gorham, Charles. *The Gilded Hearse.* New York: Creative Age Press, 1948.

Gray, Stella. *Abnormals Anonymous.* Fresno, CA: National Library Books, 1964.

Gregory, Harry. *Lesbian Web of Evil.* North Hollywood, CA: Brandon House, 1969.

Guerin, E[lsa] J[ane]. *Mountain Charley.* New York: Ballantine Books, 1968.

Hall, Radclyffe. *The Well of Loneliness.* New York: Perma Books, 1951.

Hastings, March. *Three Women.* New York: Beacon Books, 1958.

———. *The Unashamed.* New York: Midwood, 1968.

Holliday, Don. *The Man from C.A.M.P.* San Diego, CA: Corinth Publications, 1966.

———. *The Sin Travellers.* N.p.: Nightstand Books, 1962.

———. *The Stranger at the Door.* San Diego, CA: Phenix Publishers, 1967.

Hollingsworth, Elaine. *Zulma.* New York: Warner Books, 1974.

Hoyer, Neils. *Man into Woman.* New York: Popular Library Edition, 1953.

Ilton, Paul. *The Last Days of Sodom and Gomorrah.* New York: SignetBooks/NAL, 1957.

Ives, Morgan [Marion Zimmer Bradley]. *Knives of Desire.* San Diego, CA: Corinth Publications, 1966.

Jackson, Charles. *The Fall of Valor.* New York: Lion Books, 1955.

James, Anthony. *The Abnormal World of Transvestites and Sex Changes.* New York: L.S. Publications, 1965.

Jay, Victor. *AC-DC Lover.* North Hollywood, CA: Private Edition Books, 1965.

———. *So Sweet, So Soft, So Queer.* North Hollywood, CA: Private Edition Books, 1965.

Jorgensen, Christine. *A Personal Autobiography.* New York: Bantam Books, 1968.

Kapelner, Alan. *Lonely Boy Blues.* New York: Lion Books, 1956.

Kosloff, Myron. *Dial "P" for Pleasure.* Cleveland, OH: Connoisseur Publications, 1964.

Laurence, Will. *The Go Girls.* Darby, CT: Monarch Books, 1963.

Le Guin, Ursala K. *The Left Hand of Darkness.* New York: Ace Books, 1976 (orig. pub.1969).

Leigh, Michael. *The Velvet Underground.* New York: McFadden Books, 1963.

Le Mans, Vivian. *Take My Tool.* Los Angeles: Classic Publications, 1968.

Lindop, Audry Erskine. *The Tormented.* New York: Popular Library, 1956.

Linkletter, Eve. *The Gay Ones.* Fresno, CA: Fabian Books, 1958.

———. *Taxi Dancers.* Fresno, CA: Fabian Books, 1958.

Long, Frank Belknap. *Woman From Another Planet*. N.p.: Chariot Books, 1960.

Lord, Sheldon [Lawrence Block]. *69 Barrow Street*. New York, Tower Publications, 1959.

Lukas, M. J. [Doris Wishman]. *Let Me Die a Woman*. New York: Rearguard Productions, 1978.

Maine, Charles Eric [David McIlwain]. *World Without Men*. New York: Ace Books, 1958.

Manning, Bruce. *Triangle of Sin*. New York: Designs Publishing, 1952.

Mansfield, Martin. *Odd Couple*. Las Vegas, NV: Neva Paperbacks, 1967.

Marlowe, Kenneth. *A Madams Memoirs* [sic]. Chicago: Novel Books, 1965.

Marvin, Ronn. *Mr. Ballerina*. Evanston, IL: Regency Books, 1961.

Maugham, W. Somerset. *Stranger in Paris*. New York: Bantam Books, 1949.

McAlmon, Robert. *There Was a Rustle of Black Silk Stockings*. New York: Belmont Books, 1963.

McCullers, Carson. *Seven*. New York: Bantam, 1954.

McKernan, Maureen. *The Amazing Crime and Trial of Leopold and Loeb*. New York: Signet Books, 1957.

Meeker, Richard [Forman Brown]. *Torment*. New York: Universal Publication and Distribution, 1951 (orig. pub 1933 as *Better Angel*).

Michaels, Rea. *Cloak of Evil*. New York: Lancer Books, 1965.

———. *Duet in Darkness*. New York: Lancer Books, 1965.

Midre-Pagnor, John. *Sexless Lovers*. Cleveland, OH: Classics Library, 1968.

Miller, Marcus. *The Flesh Happening*. San Diego, CA: Phenix Publishers, 1967.

Moore, Alvin. *TV Guy*. N.p.: Utopia Publications, 1975.

Morgan, Clare [Patricia Highsmith]. *The Price of Salt*. New York: Bantam, 1953.

Morgan, Helene. *Queer Daddy*. San Diego, CA: Satan Press, 1965.

Morgan, Lou. *Hangout for Queers*. Las Vegas, NV: Neva Paperbacks, 1965.

Mortimer, Lee. *Women Confidential*. New York: Paperback Library, 1961.

Niles, Blair. *Strange Brother*. New York: Avon Publishing, 1952.

North, Gene. *Skid Row Sweetie*. San Diego, CA: Phenix Publishers, 1968.

Packer, Vin [Marijane Meaker]. *Whisper His Sin*. Greenwich, CT: Fawcett Publications, 1954.

Park, Jordan [Cyril Kornbluth]. *Half*. New York: Lion Books, 1953.

Peck, Oscar. *Sex Life of a Cop*. Fresno, CA: Saber Books, 1959.

Peters, Fritz [Arthur A. Peters]. *Finistère*. New York: Signet Books/NAL, 1952.

Priest, J. C. *Private School*. New York: Beacon Books, 1959.

Proferes, James J. *Hellbound in Leather*. Washington, DC: Guild Press, 1966.

Purdy, James. *Malcolm*. New York: Avon Publishing, 1959.

Rankin, Jill. *The Male Lesbian*. Cleveland, OH: Century Books, 1969.

Raynor, Darrell G. *A Year Among the Girls*. New York: Lancer Books, 1968.

Rechy, John. *City of Night*. New York: Grove Press, 1964.

Richards, Donna. *The Constant Urge*. New York: Lancer Books, 1966.

Scott, Michael. *The Killer Queens*. San Diego, CA: Corinth Publications, 1968.

Seaton, George John. *Isle of the Damned*. New York: Popular Library, 1952.

Shane, Mark. *The Lady was a Man*. Fresno, CA: Fabian Books, 1958.

———. *Sex Gantlet to Murder*. Fresno, CA: Fabian Books, 1955.

Sherman, Louise. *The Strange Three*. Fresno, CA: Saber Books, 1957.

Shrader, Bert. *Gay Stud's Trip*. San Diego, CA: Publisher's Export Company, 1968.

Sinnott, Peter. *Young Danny*. N.p.: Unique Books, 1966.

Spillane, Mickey. *Vengeance Is Mine*. New York: Signet Books/NAL, 1951.

Sprague, W. D. *The Lesbian in Our Society*. New York: Midwood Tower Publications, 1962.

Star, Hedy Jo. *I Changed My Sex!* N.p.: Allied/Novel Book, n.d.

Stuart, Chad. *The Erection*. San Diego, CA: Greenleaf Classics, 1972.

Sturgeon, Theodore. *Venus Plus X*. New York: Pyramid Books, 1960.

Taminoff, Sonia Tammy. *Don't Call Me Eloise, Call Me Al*. N.p.: Pixie Publications, 1973.

Taylor, Dyson. *Bitter Love*. New York: Pyramid Books, 1957.

Taylor, Valerie. *Unlike Others*. New York: Tower Publications, 1963.

Tellier, Andre. *Twilight Men*. New York: Pyramid Books, 1957 (orig. pub 1931).

Tesch, Gerald. *Never the Same Again*. New York: Pyramid Books, 1958.

Torres, Tereska. *Women's Barracks*. Greenwich, CT: Fawcett Publications, 1950.

Train, Ray. *Miss Kinsey's Report*. Cleveland, OH: Chevron Publications, 1967.

Travis, Ben. *The Strange Ones*. New York: Universal Publishing and Distribution, 1959.

Trelos, Tony. *Cindy Baby*. North Hollywood, CA: Brandon House, 1964.

Val Baker, Denys. *Strange Fulfillment*. New York: Pyramid Books, 1958.

Vidal, Gore. *The City and the Pillar*. New York: Signet Books/NAL, 1950.

Viereck, George Sylvester. *Men into Beasts*. Greenwich, CT: Fawcett Publications, 1952.

Wade, Carlson. *She-Male*. Wilmington, DE: Eros Publishing, n.d.

Walters, Lee. *The Right Bed*. Fresno, CA: Saber Books, 1959.

Whittington, Harry. *Rebel Woman*. New York: Avon Books, 1960.

Wilde, Oscar. *Teleny, or The Reverse of the Medal*. Chatsworth: Brandon Books, 1966 (orig. pub. 1893).

Wilhelm, Gale. *We Too Are Drifting*. New York: Berkley Books, 1955.

Williams, J. X. *AC-DC Stud*. San Diego, CA: Greenleaf Classics, 1967.

Williams, Tennessee. *A Streetcar Named Desire*. New York: Signet, 1951.

Willingham, Calder. *End as a Man*. New York: Avon Publishing, 1952 (orig. pub.1947).

Winslow, Ned. *Bottoms Up*. N.p.: Unique Books, 1966.

Wood, Ed, Jr. *Death of a Transvestite*. Aquora, CA: PAD Library, 1967.

Woolfe, Byron. *Bold Desires*. Fresno, CA: Saber Books, 1959.

————. *Killer in Drag*. Union City, NJ: Imperial Books, 1965.

Further Reading

Austen, Roger. *Playing the Game: The Homosexual Novel in America.* Indianapolis, IN: Bobbs-Merrill, 1977.

Bergman, David. "The Cultural Work of Gay Pulp Fiction." In *The Queer Sixties*, edited by Patricia J. Smith. New York: Routledge, 1999.

Bonn, Thomas L. *Under Cover: An Illustrated History of American Mass-Market Paperbacks.* New York: Penguin, 1982.

Bronski, Michael. *Culture Clash.* Boston: South End Press, 1984.

Davis, Kenneth. *Two-Bit Culture: The Paperbacking of America.* Boston: Houghton, 1984.

Foster, Jeannette. *Sex Variant Women in Literature.* Baltimore, MD: Diana Press, 1975 (orig. pub. 1956).

Garber, Eric, ed. "Those Wonderful Lesbian Pulps: A Roundtable Discussion." *San Francisco Bay Area Gay and Lesbian Historical Society Newsletter* 4:4 (summer, 1989) 1.

———. "Those Wonderful Lesbian Pulps: A Roundtable Discussion, Part II." *San Francisco Bay Area Gay and Lesbian Historical Society Newsletter* 4:5 (fall, 1989) 7–8.

Garber, Eric, and Lynn Paleo, eds. *Uranian Worlds: Sexual Variance in Science Fiction.* Boston: Alyson Press, 1986.

Grier, Barbara. *The Lesbian in Literature.* Tallahassee, FL: Naiad Press, 1967.

Harris, Daniel. "Transformations in Gay Male Porn." *Harvard Gay and Lesbian Review* 3:3 (summer, 1996) 18–22.

Hatton, Jackie. "The Pornographic Empire of H. Lynn Womack: Gay Political Discourse and Popular Culture, 1955–1970." *Thresholds: Viewing Culture* 7 (spring, 1993) 9–32.

Keller, Yvonne. "Pulp Politics: Strategies of Vision in Pro-Lesbian Pulp Novels, 1955–1965." In *The Queer Sixties*, edited by Patricia J. Smith. New York: Routledge, 1999.

Lucas, Don. Interview by Paul Gabriel. Transcript 97–32, Volume 2, pp. 11–16. San Francisco: Archives of the Gay, Lesbian, Bisexual, Transgender Historical Society of Northern California.

Miller, Laurence. "The 'Golden Age' of Gay and Lesbian Literature in Mainstream Mass-Market Paperbacks," *Paperback Parade* 47 (February, 1997) 37–66.

Norman, Tom. *American Gay Erotic Paperbacks: A Bibliography.* Burbank, CA: by the author, 1994.

O'Brien, Geoffrey. *Hardboiled America: Lurid Paperbacks and the Masters of Noir.* New York: Da Capo Press, expanded edition, 1997.

Schreuers, Piet. *Paperbacks, U.S.A.: A Graphic History, 1939–1959.* San Diego, CA: Blue Dolphin Books, 1981.

Server, Lee. *Over My Dead Body: The Sensational Age of the American Paperback, 1945–1955.* San Francisco: Chronicle Books, 1994.

Walters, Suzanna. "As Her Hand Crept Slowly up Her Thigh: Ann Bannon and the Politics of Pulp." *Social Text* 8:2 (1989), 83–101.

Weir, Angela, and Elizabeth Wilson. "The Greyhound Bus Station in the Evolution of Lesbian Popular Culture." In *New Lesbian Criticism,* edited by Sally Munt. New York: Columbia University Press, 1992.

Womack, H. Lynn. *1964–65 Guild Book Service Catalog.* Washington, DC: Guild Book Service, 1965.

Woods, Gregory. *A History of Gay Literature: The Male Tradition.* New Haven, CT: Yale University Press, 1998.

Yusba, Roberta. "Odd Girls and Strange Sisters: Lesbian Pulp Novels of the 1950s," *Out/Look 12* (spring, 1991) 34–37.

Zimet, Jaye. *Strange Sisters: The Art of the Lesbian Paperback, 1939–1969.* New York: Penguin Studio, 1999.

Archives and Archival Collections

GLBT Historical Society of Northern California
973 Market Street #400, San Francisco, CA 94103
Phone: 415.777.5455. www.glbthistory.org
*One of the largest, most accessible, and best-staffed archives
of gay, lesbian, bisexual, and transgender historical material in
the United States. The GLBT Historical Society houses over
one thousand queer-themed paperback books, mostly gay
male titles. Collections of special interest include the Patrick
Butler Erotica Collection and the personal papers of Eric
Garber, Don Lucas, and Roger Austen.*

James C. Hormel Gay and Lesbian Center
San Francisco Public Library, Main Branch
100 Larkin Street, San Francisco CA 94102
www.sfpl.lib.ca.us.
*The Hormel Center houses the Barbara Grier/Donna McBride
Collection of lesbian paperback novels. Grier owns lesbian-
oriented Naiad Press and collected lesbian paperbacks for
decades. She wrote many of the early reviews of these books
in lesbian community publications. This was her personal collection of over nine hundred volumes. The covers have all been
scanned into a searchable on-line database viewable at
206.14.7.53/glcenter/home.htm*

Valerie Taylor Collection
www.rmc.library.cornell.edu/eguides/manuscripts/7627.
html#BIOGRAPHICAL
*Cornell University Library Special Collections Department has a
wonderful collection of materials documenting human sexual
diversity. One gem is the papers of prolific lesbian pulp author
Valerie Taylor. Manuscripts, correspondence, and biographical
materials make this a rich resource.*

Bookstore

Kayo Books
814 Post Street, San Francisco, CA 94109
Phone: (415) 749-0554
www.kayobooks.com

*One of the nation's leading purveyors of vintage paperbacks,
this small store in downtown San Francisco is a veritable muse-
um of pulp fiction and nonfiction.*

Film

*Forbidden Love: The Unashamed Stories of Lesbian Lives
(Dir. Aerlyn Weissman, 1992). A poignant, irreverent, and
rebellious documentary film about the lives of nine lesbians in
Canada during the 1950s and '60s. The film makes effective
use of pulp novel covers and tabloid headlines to paint a compelling picture of the world in which these lesbian pioneers
looked for love.*

Worldwide Web Sites

Adult Novels of Men in a Womanless World:
Gay Pulp Fiction of the 1950s and 1960s.
home.earthlink.net/~seubert/pulps/pulps.html
*David Seubert's impressively researched page is without a
doubt the best on-line resource for the history of gay men's
paperback fiction. You'll be amazed at his command of incredibly
obscure facts about long-defunct fly-by-night publishing houses.*

Center for Women's History and Culture
scriptorium.lib.duke.edu/women/pulp.html
*The Rare Book, Manuscript, and Special Collections Library of
Duke University mounted a wonderful exhibit on lesbian pulps
in the summer of 2000. This Web site is chock full of resources.*

Strange Sisters Web Page
www.penguinputnam.com/strangesisters/home.htm
*This is the companion site for Jaye Zimet's book of lesbian paper-
back cover art. It has tons of links to dealers and bookstores.*

Pulp.chat
www.ThePulp.Net/index.html
*This is one of the best general sites devoted to pulp paperback
history, collecting, and lore. It's not queer-specific, but if you
cruise around the chat area you're sure to find somebody with
common interests.*

Index

Aday, Sanford, 19, 22, 24, 89, 93
Addams, Kay, 61
Adlon, Arthur, 66, 89, 92
Aldrich, Ann, 55, 57–58
Amory, Richard, 116, 117
Anderson, Jerry, 89
Archer, Marion, 42
Armory, Ricardo, 116
Austin, Roger, 100
Avati, James, 76

Baker, Denys Val, 30, 32
Baker, Dorothy, 52
Baldwin, James, 104
Bannon, Ann, 61
Barr, James, 107, 108
Barstead, Harry, 71
Berg, Louis, 46
Better Angel (Brown), 100, 101
bisexuality
    in cover art, 36
    as "first step," 29
    themes in, 45–46
    theories of, 28
Blake, Bob, 45
Block, Lawrence, 66, 68–69
Bowles, Paul, 17, 103
Box, Edgar, 17
Bradley, Marion Zimmer, 17, 56, 57, 58
Brandon House, 118
Brent, Lynton Wright, 28, 112
Britain, Sloane, 58, 61
Britt, Del, 71
Brock, Lilyan, 52
Brown, Forman, 32, 33, 100, 103
Brown, Geoff, 88, 89
Brown, Wenzell, 66
Bukowski, Charles, 89

Burns, John Horne, 103
Burroughs, William, 17

Cain, James, 12, 13
Capote, Truman, 6, 14, 17, 103
Carr, Jay, 66
Caroll, Dick, 57
Chauncey, George, 98
Christian, Paula, 61, 65
Clifton, Bud, 19, 23
Coccinelle, 82, 85
Cole, Stark, 93
Coleman, Lonnie, 104
Colton, James, 32, 33, 107
Corley, Carl, 94, 118
Costa, Mario, 82
covers
    heterosexualization of, 32
    peephole, 6, 7
    visual vocabulary of, 36
Cowell, Roberta, 82, 83
Crane, Clarkson, 12, 13
cross-dressing, 77, 85
Culver, Ed, 107

Damon, Gene, 58
Daudet, Alphonse, 52
Davidson, Chris, 108, 117
Delaney, Samuel, 17, 20
Devlin, Barry, 30
Douglas, Dean, 32, 33
Douglas, Ray, Jr., 114
Dowd, Harrison, 102, 103
du Maurier, Daphne, 52
Dunn, Mark, 118

Elbe, Lili, 74, 76
Ellis, Havelock, 50

Emerson, Jill, 66, 68, 69
Engstrand, Stuart, 76, 77
Erickson, Reed, 82
Erlich, J. W., 36
erotic realism, 36
Essex House, 89
Evans, Donald, 111
Evans, John, 52

Farmer, Phillip Jose, 89
Fawcett Books, 54, 57
Fenster, Percy, 43
Fleming, Ian, 12
Flora, Fletcher, 66, 68

Gathings Committee, 51
Gautier, Theophile, 52
gay paperbacks
    lesbian vs., 97–98
    PBOs, 104, 107, 109
    reprints, 98, 100, 103–4, 107
The Gilded Hearse (Gorham), 12, 14
Ginsberg, Allen, 17
Gorham, Charles, 12, 14
Gray, Stella, 42
Greenleaf Classics, 109, 117–18
Gregory, Harry, 71
Grier, Barbara, 58
Guerin, Elsa Jane, 87
Guild Press, 109

Half (Park), 74, 75
Hall, Radclyffe, 50
Hammett, Dashiell, 7
Hastings, March, 61, 62
Hellman, Lillian, 54
Hemingway, Ernest, 11, 12, 54
Highsmith, Patricia, 58

Hitchcock, Alfred, 9
Hitt, Orrie, 61
Hogan, Lou, 19
Holliday, Don, 39, 41, 66, 111, 114
Hollingsworth, Elaine, 87
homosexuality
    attitudes toward, 98
    military and, 11
    propaganda against, 46
    as "social problem," 9, 11
House Un-American Activities
    Committee, 54
Hoyer, Niels, 74, 76

Ilton, Paul, 5
Ives, Morgan, 56

Jackson, Charles, 14, 103
James, Antony, 81
Jay, Victor, 39, 41
Jorgensen, Christine, 73–74, 77, 82
juvenile delinquent genre, 42, 45

Kapelner, Alan, 30
Karp, David, 107
Kerouac, Jack, 17
Kerr, M. E., 55, 57
Kinsey, Alfred, 10, 11, 27
Kornbluth, Cyril, 74, 75
Kosloff, Myron, 40, 41
Kronhausen, Eberhard and Phyllis, 36

Ladder, 58
Lait, Jack, 61
Laurence, Will, 45
Lawton, Jeff, 118
Le Guin, Ursula K., 89, 90
Leigh, Michael, 45–46, 47

Le Mans, Vivian, 87
Leopold and Loeb murder trial, 9
lesbian paperbacks
    beginning of golden age of, 49, 51–52
    for a male audience, 61, 66, 70
    nonfiction, 61
    PBOs, 12, 49, 54, 57, 61
    reprints, 52, 54
    role of, in paperback trade, 12
    by women writers, 49, 51–52, 54,
        57–58, 61, 63
Let Me Die a Woman (Lukas), 81, 82
Levenson, Lew, 107, 109
Levin, Meyer, 9, 49
Lindop, Audry Erskine, 34
Linkletter, Eve, 25
Long, Frank Belknap, 17
Lord, Sheldon, 66, 68, 69
Love, Richard, 116
Lukas, M. J., 81, 82

Maine, Charles Eric, 18, 19
Man into Woman (Hoyer), 74, 76, 77
Manning, Bruce, 34
Mansfield, Martin, 45
Manutius, Aldus, 5
Marchal, Lucie, 52
Marlowe, Kenneth, 85
Marvin, Ronn, 107
Maugham, W. Somerset, 8, 11, 12, 103
Maupin, Armistead, 89
Maxey, Wallace de Ortega, 19, 22
McAlmon, Robert, 11, 12
McCullers, Carson, 14, 17
McIlwain, David, 18
McKernan, Maureen, 9
Meaker, Marijane, 55, 57–58, 107
Meeker, Richard, 32, 33, 98, 100

Michaels, Rea, 61, 64, 65
Midre-Pagnor, John, 81, 82
Miller, Laurence, 52
Miller, Marcus, 45
Moore, Alvin, 95
Morgan, Claire, 58
Morgan, Helene, 94
Morgan, Lou, 36, 37
Mortimer, Lee, 61

Nana (Zola), 51
Niles, Blair, 97, 98, 100
Norman, Tom, 107
North, Gene, 112

obscenity laws, 14, 19, 22, 24, 97, 98,
    109, 110. See also pornography

Packer, Vin, 55, 57, 107
paperbacks. See also individual genres
    characteristics of, 5
    as cultural unconscious, 7–8
    origins of, 5, 7
    sexuality and, 8
Park, Jordan, 75
PBOs
    gay, 104, 107, 109
    lesbian, 12, 49, 54, 57, 61
Peck, Oscar, 25
Peters, Fritz, 32, 33
pornography, 36, 41, 51, 97, 109, 110,
    115, 117–18. See also obscenity laws
Priest, J. C., 71
Publisher's Export Company, 118
Purdy, James, 104

"queer," meaning of, 37, 41

Rand, Lou, 19
Rankin, Jill, 81
Raynor, Darrell G., 85
Rechy, John, 89, 90
Renault, Mary, 52
Rice, Elmer, 52
Richards, Donna, 62
Ronald, James, 52

Salem, Randy, 61
San Francisco, 11, 12, 19, 23, 89
science fiction, 17, 19, 89
Scott, Michael, 114
Seaton, George John, 99
Selby, Hubert, Jr., 89
Server, Lee, 57
sexuality
    paperbacks and, 8
    studies of, 11
Shane, Mark, 89, 92, 93
The Sheltering Sky (Bowles), 17
Sherman, Louise, 34
Shrader, Bert, 118
Sinnott, Peter, 111
The Sling and the Arrow (Engstrand),
    76, 77–78, 81
Smith, Artemis, 61
Song of the Loon (Amory), 116, 117
Southern writers, 14, 17
Spillane, Mickey, 78, 79, 81
Sprague, W. D., 58, 61
Spring Fire (Packer), 57
Star, Hedy Jo, 85
Stearns, Jess, 61
Stein, Gertrude, 11, 12
Stewart, Sam, 117
Stine, Hank, 89
Stonewall Riots, 89, 117

Strange Brother (Niles), 97, 100
Stuart, Chad, 111
Sturgeon, Theodore, 17, 20
Suplee, Zelda, 82
Swados, Felice, 52
swinger fiction, 45–46

Taminoff, Sonia Tammy, 95
Taylor, Dyson, 29, 107
Taylor, Valerie, 58
Tellier, André, 98, 100, 101
Tesch, Gerald, 104
Thayer, Ann, 61
Torres, Tereska, 49, 52
Train, Ray, 10
transgender-related paperbacks
    as autobiographies or biographies,
        74, 81–82, 85, 86
    literary, 89
    origins of, 73–74, 77
    sleaze, 89, 92–95
    staple themes in, 77–78, 81
Travis, Ben, 30
Trelos, Tony, 71
Twilight Men (Tellier), 100, 101

The Velvet Underground (Leigh),
    45–46, 47
Vengeance Is Mine (Spillane), 78,
    79, 81
Vidal, Gore, 14, 17, 89, 103
Viereck, George, 104, 107

Wade, Carlson, 82, 85
Walters, Lee, 29
Wegener, Einar, 74, 76
The Well of Loneliness (Hall), 50, 52
We Too Are Drifting (Wilhelm), 52,

53, 54
Whittington, Harry, 66
Wilde, Oscar, 107, 108
Wilhelm, Gale, 52, 53, 54
Williams, J. X., 39, 41
Williams, Tennessee, 14, 17
Willingham, Calder, 30
Winston, Daoma, 27
Wishman, Doris, 81, 82
Womack, H. Lynn, 109
Women's Barracks (Torres), 49, 51,
    52, 54
Wood, Ed, Jr., 77
Woolfe, Byron, 25

Zola, Emile, 51